CONTENTS

Contents in detail

CHAPTER 6
Exceptions, Interrupts and the Job Scheduler
Exceptions — RAM exception vectors — writing exception handlers — interrupt level 2, gap interrupt, interface interrupt, transmit interrupt, frame interrupt — the polled list — the scheduler — the scheduler list — external interrupts.

CHAPTER 7
QDOS Utilities
The real-time clock, the SDATE calculations — message printing routines, error messages — base conversions, conversions to and from ASCII — memory usage, common heap allocation, linked lists, string comparison.

CHAPTER 8
Extending SuperBASIC
SuperBASIC memory map, name table, name list, variable list — adding procedures and functions — getting parameters — the maths stack — returning values — SuperBASIC channels, CAT procedure, QDOS$ function — correcting the CALL bug — floating point routines — Super-BASIC memory allocation.

CHAPTER 9
External ROMs and Device Drivers
The ROM socket — the peripheral ROMs — ROM header format — peripheral ROM problem — device drivers — simple device drivers, linking a device driver, access layer, channel open, channel close, channel I/O — queue handling — directory device driver, access layer, channel open, close and input/ output, forced slaving, format routine.

Introduction

This book is for those readers who know 68000/8 machine code, and who wish to put their knowledge to practical use on the Sinclair QL. To do this effectively, an accurate and useful guide to the QL's operating system, QDOS, is required, and this book is intended to be that guide. It is a follow-on to my previous book, *Assembly Language Programming on the Sinclair QL* (Sunshine Books, 1984), though I have tried to avoid repetition wherever possible.

This book is not just a re-hash of the 'official' Sinclair QDOS manual, as there are more than enough of these already, but takes the basic information and then extends it to give a broader understanding of QDOS and how best to use it. I wrote the book by starting with the QDOS manual and, in conjunction with various QL disassemblies, going through the ROM to work out how its various components work, to pass the knowledge on to the reader. I have not described the QDOS traps in numerical order, but in a more logical order based on their use.

I would like to express my sincere thanks to Sinclair Research for their technical assistance, and Apple for teaching Macintosh about Me. I would also like to apologise to Sunshine for the rather late arrival of this manuscript!

Andrew Pennell
Woodford Green, Essex
December 1984

CHAPTER 1
Introduction to QDOS

The history of QDOS

In January 1984 Sinclair Research launched the QL, the first home computer to offer 32-bit processing at a reasonable price. The machine's hardware was based around the Motorola 68008, and the firmware fell broadly into two sections — SuperBASIC, and the operating system. Although no-one knew it at the time, the QDOS operating system was not complete, and an alternative OS was shown at the press launch, which has since evolved into 68K OS by GST. In addition, SuperBASIC was in a very poor state at the time, and the problems associated with this, combined with production problems on the hardware, resulted in a three-month delay before the first machines were released.

Originally SuperBASIC was to be loaded from cartridge into RAM, with 32K of ROM space allocated to the firmware. However, it was later decided to put SuperBASIC on to ROM, too. As this needed about 10K more, the first machines were released with a 'kludge', containing a 16K EPROM, sticking out of the back. The in-house name for the operating system was originally 'Domestos', which as you know kills 99% of all known bugs dead! As lead times on ROMs are long, everything was on EPROM for the following few months and, so that you could tell which version you had, a VER$ function was included which revealed a two-letter code. The first such release was FB, closely followed by PM, and these contained QDOS version 1.01. Both of these had been finished very rapidly and hardly tested, and as a result these machines were full of serious bugs, both in SuperBASIC and in QDOS. The bad press the machine received when it finally appeared is due, in part at least, to the poor state of this firmware.

The next released version was AH, still on EPROM, but a larger EPROM so that the kludge could be disposed of. This contained QDOS version 1.02, which was a great improvement, both in its SuperBASIC and QDOS sections. The whole machine was much more reliable, and many extra features had been added for the machine code programmer to use. This was to be the 'final' version, but the programmers were not satisfied and a few minor changes were made before releasing version JM, the first firmware release to be put on to ROM, containing QDOS 1.03. This is the 'current' operating system, and this book is based on it: to most intents and purposes, 1.03 is exactly the same as 1.02. QDOS 1.01 is

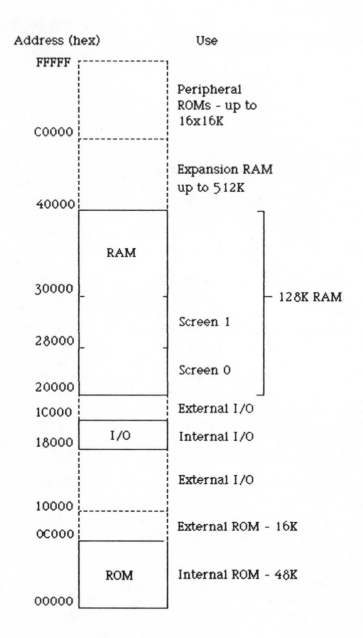

Figure 1.1: Hardware Memory Map.

totally obsolete, and shall not be mentioned again, as all such machines should have been upgraded. It is intended that this book shall be periodically updated to allow for subsequent versions of QDOS. Where known, features expected in subsequent versions of QDOS will be explained.

QL memory organisation

The controlling factor on the memory usage on the QL is the hardware memory map, shown in **Figure 1.1**.

I/O memory map

The internal I/O area starts at $18000. Due to the incomplete method of decoding used, it stretches up to $1BFFF, though there are only 10 actual ports in the QL. All are byte-sized unless otherwise stated. The usage of each is as follows:

PORT	NAME	USE
$18000	PC.CLOCK	long word for real-time clock in seconds
$18002	PC.TCTRL	transmit control
$18003	PC.IPCWR	IPC port: write only
$18020	PC.IPCRD	IPC port: read only
$18020	PC.MCTRL	microdrive control register: write only
$18021	PC.INTR	interrupt register
$18022	PC.TDATA	transmit register: write only
$18022	PC.TRAK1	microdrive read track 1
$18023	PC.TRAK2	microdrive read track 2
$18063	MC.STAT	master chip status register

Most of these cannot usefully be accessed by programs, but there are two exceptions.

The clock long word is normally read only, containing the time and date in seconds. Writing directly to the port will usually cause it to reset to 0. To set the value of the clock, it is best to use the relevant system trap. The clock is set by writing a rotating binary mask into the register, the exact details of which are not important. The time of $00000000 corresponds to January 1, 1961, 00:00:00. There are various system routines to convert the time in seconds into a more usable form.

The master chip status register is write only, and controls the screen mode, with three bits:

bit 1   when set turns screen display off
bit 3   set for 8-colour mode, reset for 4-colour
bit 7   reset for screen#0 at $20000, set for screen#1 at $28000

Under QDOS a copy of the register is stored at SV.MCSTA, at $28034.

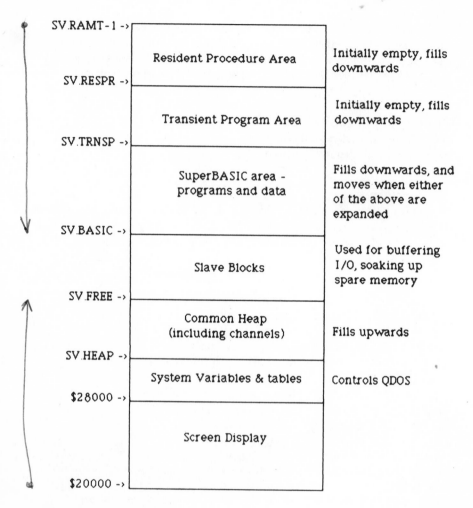

Figure 1.2:   RAM Memory Map.

RAM memory map

The standard machine has 128K RAM, but this can be increased in 64K steps up to 640K. There is an unfortunate disadvantage in using the internal RAM for machine code — due to the way in which the RAM is refreshed by a ULA, RAM accesses are very much slower than they should be, resulting in a greatly reduced speed of program execution. However, this disadvantage does not apply to ROMs (internal or external) or to external RAM. The RAM memory map under QDOS is shown in **Figure 1.2**.

System variables

Some $180 bytes are reserved for use by the system for holding certain important information, especially pointers to the various system tables. Current versions of QDOS do not use all of the allocated space, with $80 bytes available to user programs. However, the 'unused' status of these bytes is not guaranteed for subsequent versions of QDOS. The system variables are summarised below, in decimal and hexadecimal, and by their official mnemonic where known.

163840	$28000	SV.IDENT	long	identification word, $D254
163844	$28004	SV.CHEAP	long	start of common heap
163848	$28008	SV.CHPFR	long	first free space in common heap
163852	$2800C	SV.FREE	long	start of free area
163856	$28010	SV.BASIC	long	start of SuperBASIC area
163860	$28014	SV.TRNSP	long	start of transient program area
163864	$28018	SV.TRNFR	long	first free area in TRNSP
163868	$2801C	SV.RESPR	long	start of resident procedure area
163872	$28020	SV.RAMT	long	end of RAM+1 (=$40000 for 128K)
163876	$28024		10 bytes unused	
163886	$2802E	SV.RAND	word	psuedo-random number
163888	$28030	SV.POLLM	word	number of poll interrupts missed
163890	$28032	SV.TVMOD	byte	0 monitor, <>0 TV — (corrupted by SuperBASIC MODE command)
163891	$28033	SV.SCRST	byte	0 screen active, <> 0 inactive, toggled by pressing CTRL F5
163892	$28034	SV.MCSTA	byte	copy of TV register (MC.STAT)
163893	$28035	SV.PCINT	byte	copy of interrupt register (PC.INTR)
163894	$28036		byte	not used
163895	$28037	SV.NETNR	byte	network station number 1–64 (default=1)
163896	$28038	SV.I2LST	long	start of external interrupt list
163900	$2803C	SV.PLIST	long	start of polled tasks list
163904	$28040	SV.SHLST	long	start of scheduler tasks list
163908	$28044	SV.DRLST	long	start of simple device driver list
163912	$28048	SV.DDLST	long	start of directory driver list
163916	$2804C	SV.KEYQ	long	current keyboard queue (0 if none)
163920	$28050	SV.TRAPV	long	current RAM vector table (0 if none)
163924	$28054	SV.BTPNT	long	most recent slave block entry
163928	$28058	SV.BTBAS	long	start of slave block table
163932	$2805C	SV.BTTOP	long	end of slave block table
163936	$28060	SV.JBTAG	word	current value of job tag
163938	$28062	SV.JBMAX	word	highest job number to date
163940	$28064	SV.JBPNT	long	current job table entry
163944	$28068	SV.JBBAS	long	start of job table
163948	$2806C	SV.JBTOP	long	end of job table
163952	$28070	SV.CHTAG	word	current value of channel tag
163954	$28072	SV.CHMAX	word	highest channel number to date
163956	$28074	SV.CHPNT	long	last channel checked by the waiting I/O scheduler routine
163960	$28078	SV.CHBAS	long	start of channel table

(handwritten margin notes: "Memory Areas", "List Addresses", "Slave Blocks", "Jobs", "Channels")

163964	$2807C	SV.CHTOP	long	end of channel table
163968	$28080		8 bytes unused	
163976	$28088	SV.CAPS	word	caps lock: 0 off, $FF00 on
163978	$2808A	SV.ARBUF	word	last key pressed
163980	$2808C	SV.ARDEL	word	key repeat delay (normally 30)
163982	$2808E	SV.ARFRQ	word	key repeat frequency (normally 4)
163984	$28090	SV.ARCNT	word	key repeat counter
163986	$28092	SV.CQCH	word	change keyboard queue code (normally 3=CTRL C)
163988	$28094	SV.WP	word	should be write-protect status of microdrives, but not implemented
163990	$28096	SV.SOUND	word	sound status: 0 off, $FF00 on
163992	$28098	SV.SER1C	long	address of serial port 1 input queue
163996	$2809C	SV.SER2C	long	address of serial port 2 input queue
164000	$280A0	SV.TMODE	byte	ULA transmit mode: bits 0–2: baud rate number bit 3: 0 ser1, 1 ser2 bit 4: microdrive turning
164002	$280A2	SV.CSUB	long	routine to call when CAPS LOCK is held down (0 if none)
164006	$280A6	SV.TIMO	word	counter for timing serial output
164008	$280A8	SV.TIMOV	word	value of above timeout (=1200/baud +1)
164010	$280AA	SV.FSTAT	word	cursor flash counter
164012	$280AC		66 bytes unused	
164078	$280EE	SV.MDRUN	byte	currently turning microdrive
164079	$280EF	SV.MDCNT	byte	microdrive counter
164080	$280F0	SV.MDDID	8 bytes	drive ID*4 for every drive
164088	$280F8	SV.MDSTA	8 bytes	status of each drive
164096	$28100	SV.FSDEF	16 long	pointers to physical definitions
164160	$28140	SV.STACB	192 long	lowest position for SSP
164992	$28480	SV.STACT		highest position for SSP

On first reading the above table, a lot of it won't mean much to you unless you're already familiar with QDOS, but most of the meanings are all explained somewhere in this book. This table is the only one to contain any decimal information, as some variables can be usefully accessed from SuperBASIC. All other addresses will be given in hex only, as five-digit hex numbers translate into very forgettable and easily mis-typeable decimal numbers. As with all QDOS constants, the system variable names consist of two parts — usually a two-letter prefix, followed by a longer name. Different types of constants have different prefixes, summarised here:

MT	manager trap	BP	BASIC procedure
JB	jobs	SV	system variable
IO	input/output	CH	channels
Q	queues	FS	file system

PC	peripheral chip	MC	master chip
MD	microdrive	SD	screen display
NET	network	SER	serial ports
BV	BASIC system variables	RI	arithmetic
MM	memory management	CN	conversions
UT	utility	CA	convert parameters

When writing your own programs you can usually omit the two-letter prefix — though there are some similar names that could get misinterpreted, such as JB.TRAPV and SV.TRAPV which would be ambiguous without their prefixes.

Supervisor stack

The system stack pointer (SSP) always lies in the area shown in Figure 1.2, with its base at $28480, up (or down, if you see what I mean!) to $28140. Note that no checks are ever made on the value of the SSP, but under normal programming the $300 bytes is room enough.

Common heap

This is a special heap, used mainly by channels, but which can also be used by jobs for storing data. It is a general workspace area; each time a section is allocated, QDOS keeps track of which job allocated it so that, when the job is removed, those parts of the heap can be reclaimed and other jobs can use them. If many jobs request heap space, it can become very fragmented, and it is best for jobs to request a large data space when created, then set up their own heaps using the data space allocated.

The common heap is allocated in multiples of eight bytes, and each section is preceded by a 16-byte header, in the form of four long words: the first is the length of the block; the second is either the address of the I/O driver to free the block, or a pointer to the next free space; the third is the ID of the owner job; while the fourth is an address to be set when the space is released.

Slave blocks

This is an area of memory which expands to fill the free space, used by the microdrives for storing copies of sectors, to speed up their operations.

SuperBASIC area

This is an area containing SuperBASIC's own system variables, its program, actual variables, and the tables necessary for its operation. Every-

7

thing within the area is accessed relative to A6 (explained in Chapter 8) because the whole area is likely to move up and down when space is allocated in RESPR or TRNSP. Writing software to add to SuperBASIC is also covered in Chapter 8.

Transient program area — TRNSP

After a switch-on, this area is empty. It expands to make room for jobs, their headers, and data areas.

Resident procedure area — RESPR

This is the very top of RAM and normally on switch-on it is empty (it may not be empty if an external ROM is connected). It expands to hold extra procedures or functions to be used from SuperBASIC (hence the name), and for general machine code that is to be executed from SuperBASIC. This area can only be allocated or released when TRNSP is empty, as jobs (except SuperBASIC) cannot be relocated, as would be necessary. While RESPR can be expanded in stages, it can only be contracted in one step, by totally collapsing the area. This latter operation can be rather dangerous, though, as the area may contain QDOS links or extensions that will crash the machine if removed.

Screen memory

This takes up 32K, and under QDOS it lies at $20000. Its exact layout is shown in **Figure 1.3**.

Calling QDOS routines

Approximately half of the QL's ROM is devoted to QDOS and, for the programmer to access the most useful parts, certain entry points have been provided that ensure upward compatibility with subsequent versions of the ROM. There are two ways of calling QDOS — via system traps or system vectors.

System traps

Traps #0 to #4 inclusive are reserved for QDOS calls thus:

TRAP #0   enters supervisor mode
TRAP #1   general manager traps, particularly memory and job control
TRAP #2   input/output allocation traps
TRAP #3   actual I/O including graphics and file handling
TRAP #4   special trap for the BASIC interpreter

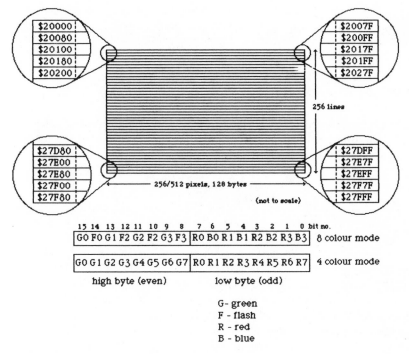

15 14 13 12 11 10 9 8	7 6 5 4 3 2 1 0 bit no.	
G0 F0 G1 F2 G2 F2 G3 F3	R0 B0 R1 B1 R2 B2 R3 B3	8 colour mode
G0 G1 G2 G3 G4 G5 G6 G7	R0 R1 R2 R3 R4 R5 R6 R7	4 colour mode
high byte (even)	low byte (odd)	

G- green
F - flash
R - red
B - blue

Figure 1.3:   Usual Screen Memory Map.

Traps #0 and #4 have no parameters, but the rest have a standard register usage, which involves D0 selecting the function on entry. Parameters are passed to the routines in registers D1–D3 and A0–A3, with an error number returned in D0. Error numbers are negative long words, starting at 0 for no error, then −1 for 'not complete', and so on for all the errors (see Appendix B). The registers corrupted by the traps vary from function to function, detailed under each description, but, with a few exceptions, registers D4–D7 and A4–A7 are never corrupted.

System vectors

The other way of accessing QDOS is by using certain word-sized vectors stored just after the exception table, starting at $000C0. Parameters are usually passed via the same registers as traps, though the value of D0 is usually irrelevant on entry. The normal way of accessing these vectors is via indirect addressing so, for example, vector $C4 could be called with:

MOVE.W $00C4,A4   read vector
JSR   (A4)   call routine

9

However, some routines cannot be reached with a word-sized vector, and require $4000 to be added to them, so calling vector $124 could be done with:

```
MOVE.W      $0124,A4
JSR         $4000(A4)
```

Usually system calls are handled like any other subroutines, but some have multiple return locations, depending on the results of the routine, and may require a section of code similar to:

```
JSR         (A4)        call it
BRA.S       BIT1        1st return point
BRA.S       BIT2        2nd return point
BRA.S       BIT3        3rd return point
```

Most routines return an error number in register D0, either in the form of a long negative word, or 0 if there are no errors (thus TST.L D0 can tell if any error has occurred). It is also possible to add user-defined error messages (particularly useful for external device drivers) by putting the start address of the message in D0, and then setting bit 31. The error should start with a word defining its length, followed by the actual ASCII, and ending in an LF byte.

System routines divide into two groups — atomic, and non-atomic. Atomic routines can be called in supervisor mode, while non-atomic ones must not. Unless otherwise stated, all QDOS routines are atomic.

SuperBASIC machine code support
Although it could not be said that SuperBASIC is the most ideal environment for entering and executing machine code, it is better than nothing, and has the following machine code related keywords:

RESPR
This is a function that reserves space in the resident procedure space above SuperBASIC, used with a number in brackets denoting how many bytes are required (which is internally rounded up to a multiple of eight). The result of the function is the location of the first address created. It has two possible error returns — either 'out of memory', or 'not complete' if any jobs are present in the system other than SuperBASIC. The function RESPR(0) returns the first location of the area, equivalent to reading

SV.RESPR. This is the usual area for storing machine code that is to be executed from SuperBASIC, and procedure definitions to be added to the system.

CALL

This is a procedure that executes machine code as a subroutine. It should be followed by an address and, optionally, up to 13 numeric parameters. These parameters get placed into registers D1–D7/A0–A5 in that order. On entry to the specified routine, D0 is set to –15, which signals a 'bad parameter' error. To return to SuperBASIC, D0 must be zeroed and an RTS done. The routine will be executed in user mode, and A6 should not be altered within the routine. Note that in all existing versions of the ROM there is a fatal bug in this routine that can cause the machine to crash with a large SuperBASIC program present. The method for correcting it is given in Chapter 8. In addition, if the starting address is odd, the command will be completely ignored, to avoid causing an address error.

SBYTES

This is a procedure for saving sections of code on to a device. Its general syntax is:

SBYTES <device>, <start address>, <number of bytes>

where all the parameters are mandatory. The routine saves the bytes on to the specified device, along with a header containing the length only (ie the start address is *not* saved in the header).

LBYTES

This is the opposite of the above, of the general form:

LBYTES <device>, <start address>

and, because SBYTES doesn't save the start address, this *must* be specified in the command.

SEXEC

This is a procedure for generating program files (usually on microdrive) that can be loaded as multi-tasking jobs. Its general form is:

SEXEC <device>, <start address>, <length>, <data space>

11

where all parameters are mandatory. The meaning of 'data space' is covered in the next chapter. A file created using SEXEC can be loaded using LBYTES, though it will not execute. Note that the start address is not saved along with the bytes.

EXEC_W
This is a procedure for loading files created with SEXEC, and executing them as jobs. It has the general form:

EXEC_W <device>

and will load the file from the device into the transient program area, then execute it concurrently with any other jobs in the system. When it has finished, control will return to SuperBASIC. An attempt to EXEC a file that was created with an operation other than SEXEC will produce the error 'bad parameter'. Present versions of SuperBASIC do not support multiple device names in one command, or process names, as described in the first edition of the QL User Guide.

EXEC
This is the same as EXEC_W, except that control will return immediately to SuperBASIC, with the job running concurrently.

POKE
There are three forms of this for the different data sizes, these being POKE, POKE_W and POKE_L, followed by the address and then the data to be POKEd, of appropriate size. For _W and _L versions, the address must be even.

PEEK
This is the opposite of the above, being three functions to read memory, PEEK, PEEK_W, and PEEK_L. As above, the address must be even for the word and long-sized functions.

QDOS status trap
There is a general system trap to find information about the current state of QDOS, thus:

MT.INF — get QDOS information: TRAP #1 with D0=0

Entry: none

Exit: D1.L   current job ID (explained in Chapter 2)
D2.L   QDOS version number as ASCII string, eg '1.03'
D3   preserved
A0   start of system variables (always $28000)
A1   preserved
A2   preserved
A3   preserved

Errors: none

Action: The status of the QDOS system and jobs are returned. The 'system variables' parameter is left over from preliminary versions of QDOS which had the ability to place the system variables in an alternate position, though now they are fixed in memory.

Memory allocation traps

MT.ALRES — allocate resident procedure space: TRAP #1 with D0=$0E

Entry: D1.L   number of bytes required

Exit: D1   corrupted
D2   corrupted
D3   corrupted
A0   start of area allocated
A1   corrupted
A2   corrupted
A3   corrupted

Errors: −1   not complete as TRNSP area not empty
−3   out of memory

Action: So long as TRNSP is empty, an attempt is made to increase the resident procedure area, subject to available memory.

MT.RERES — release entire resident procedure area: TRAP #1 with D0=$0F

Entry: None

Exit:	D1	corrupted
	D2	corrupted
	D3	corrupted
	A0	corrupted
	A1	corrupted
	A2	corrupted
	A3	corrupted

Errors:	−1	transient program area not empty

Action: So long as the transient program area is empty, the resident procedure space is collapsed. The trap is extremely dangerous to use, as the area may contain links for the system or device drivers and if they are removed the system is liable to crash.

Note: In current versions of QDOS, this trap does not work reliably — it can actually allocate more space instead of collapsing it!

MT.ALCHP — allocate common heap: TRAP #1 with D0=$18

Entry:	D1.L	number of bytes required
	D2.L	owner job ID (−1 if to be owned by current job)

Exit:	D1.L	number of bytes allocated
	D2	corrupted
	D3	corrupted
	A0.L	base of area allocated
	A1	corrupted
	A2	corrupted
	A3	corrupted

Errors:	−2	invalid job ID
	−3	out of memory

Action: Memory permitting, space is allocated on the common heap to a certain job. When the job is released, all heap space used by it is reclaimed for use by other jobs. (The meaning of a job ID is explained in the next chapter.)

MT.RECHP — release common heap space: TRAP #1 with D0=$19

Entry:	A0.L	start of area to be released

Exit:	D1	corrupted
	D2	corrupted
	D3	corrupted
	A0	corrupted
	A1	corrupted
	A2	corrupted
	A3	corrupted

Errors: none

Action: The common heap space is reclaimed for use by other software. If A0 is not a valid value, the system is liable to crash.

User heaps

Programs can define their own heaps, and then use certain utilities to handle them. User heaps are allocated in multiples of eight bytes, and each section has at its start two long words — the first is the length of the space, and the second is a relative pointer to the next free space. Every section is thus linked together as a list, and the utilities do all the hard work of finding free space within them and linking it in.

MT.ALLOC — allocate area in a heap: TRAP #1 with D0=$0C

Entry:	D1.L	length of space required
	A0	pointer to pointer to free space (relative to A6)

Exit:	D1.L	amount of bytes allocated
	D2	corrupted
	D3	corrupted
	A0	start of area allocated (relative to A6)
	A1	corrupted
	A2	corrupted
	A3	corrupted

Errors: −3   no free space large enough

Action: If possible, an area is allocated in the user heap.

MT. LNKFR — link a free space (back) into a user heap: TRAP #1 with D0=$0D

Entry:	D1.L	length to link in

15

| | A0.L | base of new space (relative to A6) |
| | A1.L | pointer to pointer to free space (relative to A6) |

Exit:	D1	corrupted
	D2	corrupted
	D3	corrupted
	A0	corrupted
	A1	corrupted
	A2	corrupted
	A3	corrupted

Errors: none

Vectors $D8 (MM.ALLOC) and $DA (MM.LNKFR) are non-atomic versions of the above two routines.

CHAPTER 2
Multi-tasking

Jobs

Multi-tasking is a major feature of the QL, allowing programs to run concurrently, sharing the CPU. Normally there is only one job running, namely SuperBASIC, but the system can cater for a large number of jobs, depending on the amount of RAM. Each job can have its own program and data area, though SuperBASIC is handled slightly differently as it can change the size of its data areas.

Jobs use two main areas of RAM — there is the 'job table', just after the system variables, and the 'transient program area', which stores each job with the exception of SuperBASIC. The job table varies in size, and consists of a long word for each job. The maximum number of jobs is calculated to be ((RAM-32768)/512+32)/4, up to a maximum of 120. In the 128K machine, this corresponds to 56 jobs. Each long word holds either a pointer to the transient program area, or the long word $FF000000 if there is no entry. A job is referenced by a long word known as its ID, which has as its 'low word' a number corresponding to its position in the job table, and as its 'high word' a tag which increases by 1 each time a job is created. The first job (job 0) is SuperBASIC, which always has an ID of 0 and cannot be removed from the system. Job 0 is treated differently to other jobs by some system routines.

When space is made for a job in the transient program area, an additional $68 bytes of space are made to hold the job header. This contains various parameters for the job, as well as acting as storage for the register values of the job. The format of the job header is:

$00	JB.LEN	long	length of job area (including header)
$04	JB.START	long	start address of the job — set when job created
$08	JB.OWNER	long	the owner of this job (0 if independent)
$0C	JB.HOLD	long	location to be cleared when job removed (0 if not required)
$10	JB.TAG	word	job tag (ie high word of job ID)
$12	JB.PRIOR	byte	priority
$13	JB.PRINC	byte	priority increment (0 if inactive)
$14	JB.STAT	word	status:
			0 — possibly active
			positive — delay time until re-activation

			-1 — suspended
			-2 — waiting for another job to complete
			(no other negative values allowed)
$16	JB.RELA6	byte	bit 7 set immediately after trap #4
$17	JB.WFLAG	byte	bit 7 set if another job waiting for completion
$18	JB.WJOB	long	ID for above waiting job
$1C	JB.TRAPV	long	RAM exception vector location (or 0 if none)
$20	JB.D0	long	storage for D0
. . .	. . .	. . .	. . .
$3C	JB.D7	long	storage for D7
$40	JB.A0	long	storage for A0
. . .	. . .	. . .	. . .
$5C	JB.A7	long	storage for A7=USP (not SSP)
$60	JB.SR	word	storage for SR
$62	JB.PC	long	storage for program counter
$66		word	not used
$68	JB.END		start of actual job or data

The complete process of multi-tasking is controlled by interrupts, but it's very important to remember that *multi-tasking is only active when in user mode* and with interrupts enabled. After certain system traps called in user mode and otherwise after every frame (50 or 60 times a second) the 'scheduler' is called, which has overall control over the jobs. It sorts out which are active and when they should be enabled, using the data in the job header. When a job is deemed to have come to the end of its current timeslice, it gets suspended and its register values are copied into the job header. The scheduler then warm starts the next job, by reversing the procedure. The scheduler is rather complex, and a complete under-standing of it is not necessary, though its exact operations are covered in detail in Chapter 6.

The official QDOS documentation describes a standard method by which jobs can be given names in a defined way, though the current ver-sions of QDOS do not take any notice of them. It is not necessary for jobs to have this extended format, but it is good practice to follow it — after all, it only takes up around 20 extra bytes. Each job's name is stored starting at byte 6 of the area of the job's code space, after the header. It is in the form:

JB.END+6	word	$4AFB — identification word
JB.END+8	word	length of job name
JB.END+$A	bytes	ASCII of the name itself

As jobs normally start at JB.END, the spare six bytes should be used for a BRA or JMP instruction to skip past the job name header. The official QDOS documentation also describes certain additional information that is put on the job's stack before activation, but as current versions of QDOS do not support this, it is presumed that later versions will. The words that will be placed on the stack are: a word containing the number of channels opened for the job, followed by a suitable number of long words holding each channel ID.

Jobs have a tree-like structure, with job 0 always at the top of the tree. Job 0 owns jobs defined as independent, and can own other jobs, and in turn all jobs can each own other jobs. **Figure 2.1** shows an example of a job structure.

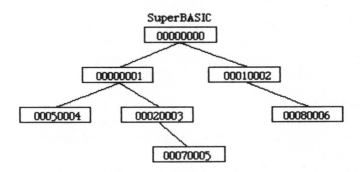

Figure 2.1:   A Typical Job Tree
IDs are examples only.

To use multi-tasking, a job must have an area created for its header and (optionally) its code and data space. The job can then be controlled to suit the application, and finally when the job is finished it can be removed. To handle all of these features there are several system traps.

Multi-tasking system traps

MT.CJOB — create a job: TRAP #1 with D0=1

Entry:	D1.L	owner job ID
	D2.L	code space required
	D3.L	data space required
	A1.L	start address

Exit:	D1.L	new job's ID
	D2	preserved
	D3	preserved
	A0.L	start of area in TRNSP allocated + $68
	A1	preserved
	A2	preserved
	A3	preserved

19

Errors: −2   invalid owner job or job table full
          −3   out of memory

Action: A job header and suitable following area are reserved in TRNSP, and an entry made in the job table. The job itself is not started. If the owner job ID is 0 then the job is independent: if the ID is negative then the job will be owned by the current job. If the start address is 0 then the address is assumed to be the first code location allocated in TRNSP, otherwise it should be specified. If the job code is to be in TRNSP, then it should always start directly after the job header, otherwise the job's start address cannot be specified. Of course, if TRNSP is used only for data or just the header, then an absolute start address can be given.

The first unused entry is searched for in the job table, and an error return made if there is no room. If there *is* room, then TRNSP is expanded by D2+D3+$68, memory permitting. The job table entry is entered, and JB.MAX updated if necessary. The entire header area from JB.START onwards is zeroed, then JB.OWNER and JB.TAG are set, and SV.JBTAG incremented. The current value of SV.TRAPV is copied into JB.TRAPV, then the initial contents of the register storage areas are set. The location of the jobs stack is set to the end of the area located, and a long word of 0 put on it. Finally contents of JB.PC and JB.START are both set to the original value of A1 (or the start of the allocated code area if A1=0).

MT.ACTIV — activate a job: TRAP #1 with D0=$0A

Entry: D1.L   job ID
          D2.B   priority (0 to 127)
          D3.W   timeout

Exit: D1   preserved
        D2   corrupted
        D3   corrupted
        A0   job header location
        A1   preserved
        A2   preserved
        A3   corrupted if D3<>0

Errors: −1   job is already active
          −2   invalid job ID

Action: The selected job has its priority set to the desired value, and is activated. If the timeout is 0 then the current job will continue executing, otherwise the current job will wait until the new job has finished (which it does by force removing itself). *This trap is not atomic, as it exits via the scheduler* unless an error occurs.

After checking for a valid job ID and that the job is not already executing, PRINC is set to the new priority, and JB.PC is set to the value of JB.START. If D3 is 0 (ie the current job is to continue) then the scheduler is entered directly, otherwise bit 7 of JB.WFLAG is set, JB.WJOB is set to the calling job, JB.STAT of the calling job is set to -2 (to indicate 'waiting'), and an exit is made via the scheduler.

When a job starts, the register values are all 0 except A4–A7. These are set up to point to potentially used areas within the job: (A6) points to the start of the code, ie JB.END, (A6,A4) points to the start of the data area, (A6,A5) points to immediately past the data area end, and A7 is A6+A5−4.

MT.PRIOR — change job priority: TRAP #1 with D0=$0B

Entry:	D1.L	job ID
	D2.B	new priority 0–127

Exit:	D1.L	preserved
	D2	preserved
	D3	preserved
	A0	job header location
	A1	preserved
	A2	preserved
	A3	preserved

Errors:	−2	invalid job ID

Action: The priority of the selected job (or the current job if D1=−1) is set to a new value — a value of 0 will make the job inactive. *This trap is not atomic as it exits via the scheduler.*

First the job header location is found, and D2 stored in PRINC. Note that no checks are made on the value of D2, so the programmer must ensure that D2 is not negative. If D2=0 (ie the job is to be made inactive) then PRIOR is zeroed, to make sure that it has no chance of executing subsequently. In either case, an exit is made via the scheduler.

MT.SUSJB — suspend a job: TRAP #1 with D0=8

Entry:	D1.L	job ID

	D3.W	timeout
	A1	address of byte to be zeroed on release

Exit:	D1.L	preserved
	D2	preserved
	D3	preserved
	A0	location of job header
	A1	preserved
	A2	preserved
	A3	preserved

Errors:	−2	invalid job ID

Action: The selected job (or the current job if D1=−1) is suspended for a period of frames. If D3=−1 then the period is indefinite. Other negative timeouts should not be specified. *This trap is not atomic as it exits via the scheduler.*

The job header location is found, D3 placed in JB.STAT, and A1 in JB.HOLD, then the scheduler is entered. No checks are made on the value of D3.

MT.RELJB — release a suspended job: TRAP #1 with D0=9

Entry:	D1.L	job ID

Exit:	D1.L	preserved
	D2	preserved
	D3	preserved
	A0	location of job header
	A1	preserved
	A2	preserved
	A3	preserved

Errors:	−2	invalid job ID

Action: A suspended job is released. *This trap is not atomic as it exits via the scheduler.*

The job header is found, and JB.STAT tested — if it is 0 (ie the job was not suspended) then the scheduler is immediately entered, else JB.STAT is zeroed, and the byte at location JB.HOLD is zeroed (provided it's not already zero), before entering the scheduler.

MT.RJOB — remove a job: TRAP #1 with D0=4

Entry:	D1.L	job ID
	D3.L	error code

Exit:	D1	corrupted
	D2	corrupted
	D3	corrupted
	A0	corrupted
	A1	corrupted
	A2	corrupted
	A3	corrupted

Errors:	−1	job is active
	−2	invalid job ID

Action: The selected job (or the current job if D1=−1) is removed from TRNSP, along with its subsidiaries, provided that the job is inactive. The activity or otherwise of the subsidiary jobs is irrelevant, so subsidiaries that are still executing will be removed regardless. Job 0 (SuperBASIC) cannot be removed. *This trap is not atomic as it can exit via the scheduler.*

After checking that it is not job 0, JB.PRINC is tested to see if the job is running, forcing an error if it's not 0 (ie it's active). Next the job tree is traversed forwards and each job found is marked, until all the subsidiaries are found. Then each marked job has JB.FLAG examined, to see if another job is waiting for it. If JB.STAT is −2 (ie it's waiting for I/O) then its JB.STAT is zeroed (to cancel the 'waiting' state), and the initial value of D3 is passed to the waiting job in D0, as an error code. The next thing is for the common heap area to be scanned, and any sections owned by the outgoing job are reclaimed (which includes any channel definition blocks owned by the job), followed by the reclamation of the area in TRNSP itself. Next the job table entry has its high byte set to $FF (to indicate 'unused'), and the process is repeated until all the subsidiaries have been removed in this way. If the current job was one of those removed, then a jump is made to the scheduler, otherwise an ordinary exit is made.

MT.FRJOB — force remove job: TRAP #1 with D0=5

Entry:	D1.L	job ID
	D3.L	error code

Exit:	D1	corrupted
	D2	corrupted

D3	corrupted
A0	corrupted
A1	corrupted
A2	corrupted
A3	corrupted

Errors: −2   invalid job ID

Action: The specified job (or the current job if D3=−1) is removed from TRNSP along with its subsidiaries, whether it is executing or not. *This trap is not atomic as it can exit via the scheduler.*

The steps taken are similar to MT.RJOB, with the exception that the contents of JB.STAT are ignored.

MT.JINF — get information on job: TRAP #1 with D0=2

Entry:	D1.L	job ID
	D2.L	ID of job at top of tree

Exit:	D1.L	next job in tree (or 0 if no more)
	D2.L	owner job ID
	D3.L	priority — negative if suspended
	A0	location of actual job (after header)
	A1	corrupted
	A2	preserved
	A3	preserved

Errors: −2   invalid job ID

Action: This trap checks the status of jobs. It can be used to traverse a complete tree of jobs by starting with D1=D2=job at top of tree, then calling the trap successively until D1=0.

First the job ID is checked, and the header location found. The location of JB.PRINC is put in the lowest byte of D3, the remaining three bytes being zeroed if the job is active, or each set to $FF if not. The next job in the tree is found, its ID put in D1, and A0 set to JB.END.

MT.FREE — find maximum amount of space for a job: TRAP #1 with D0=6

Entry: no parameters

Exit:	D1.L	maximum free space
	D2	corrupted
	D3	corrupted
	A0	corrupted
	A1	corrupted
	A2	corrupted
	A3	corrupted

Errors: none

Action: The size of the largest continuous block of free space in TRNSP (or that could be allocated to TRNSP) is found. This is useful for jobs that need to use as much memory as possible, eg a word processor. If a job of this size is created then it means that there is very little left for other jobs, or slave blocks in RAM.

First the largest amount of space in TRNSP is found, then compared with SV.BASIC−SV.FREE−$200, and D1 returns with whichever is the greater. As QDOS is a multi-tasking system, if you try to allocate a job with this much space you can't be certain that another job hasn't grabbed the space in the meantime!

Multi-tasking from SuperBASIC

EXEC and EXEC_W
These are SuperBASIC procedures for loading and executing jobs created with the SEXEC command, normally from microdrive. What they do is read the file header, allocate space for the program and data according to the header's contents, then start the job with a priority of 32, which is the same as SuperBASIC itself. They differ in that MT.ACTIV has a timeout of −1 for EXEC_W, and of 0 for EXEC.

CHAPTER 3
The 8049 Second Processor

In addition to the 68008 processor, there is a slave processor, an Intel 8049. It contains on-board ROM and RAM, which is not directly accessible from the 68008. Communication between processors is via two ports, by quite a complex protocol.

The 8049 is responsible for certain peripheral devices, namely the serial ports, the audio speaker, the keyboard. There exists a system trap that enables a certain amount of the 8049 to be used by the 68008, with 16 functions, of which some are not practical in normal circumstances and others don't seem to have any effect.

IPC command trap

MT.IPCOM — send a command to the 8049: TRAP #1 with D0=$11

Entry: A3.L pointer to command

Exit: D1.B return parameter
D2 preserved
D3 preserved
D5 corrupted (NB)
D7 corrupted (NB)
A0 preserved
A1 preserved
A2 preserved
A3 preserved

Errors: none

Action: The command is sent to the 8049, and may produce a return parameter, depending on its function. The format of the command is quite complicated, thus:

0(A3) byte determines function, from 0 to $0F
1(A3) byte number of parameters to send (up to 16)

2(A3)　　long　　defines the amount of each parameter to be sent, with two bits for each parameter, bits 0 and 1 for first parameter, bits 2 and 3 for second, and so on. This word may be left undefined only if 1(A3)=0 (ie no parameters).

6(A3)　　byte　　1st parameter

and so on for each parameter

7+n(A3)　byte　　size of reply from 8049, bits 0 and 1 (n = number of parameters)

The bits to control the amount of each parameter transmitted are

00　　least significant four bits
01　　nothing
10　　all eight bits
11　　nothing

(These bits also control the size of the reply, if any.)

Given just this information, it would be nearly impossible to do anything useful with the 8049, so it's best to use only specified commands, and these are given below.

IPC 0 — processor reset

The command is seven bytes in length, being 0 0 ? ? ? ? 1 (where ? means 'don't care'), and results in the 8049 resetting. Unfortunately this is of no use at all as it makes the QL stop processing.

IPC 1 — report input status

This is seven bytes in length, being 1 0 ? ? ? ? 2, and returns a byte-sized reply of the form:

BIT　MEANING WHEN SET
0　　if key being pressed
1　　sound is being produced
2　　undefined
3　　undefined
4　　a byte has been read from serial port 1
5　　as above but port 2
6　　the rotating cartridge is write-protected
7　　undefined

The bits marked 'undefined' should always be masked off, as they are not guaranteed to remain stable in state.

The keyboard matrix is based on a 9 × 11 grid, consisting of an 8 × 8 grid containing the normal keys, with CTRL, SHIFT and ALT being separate from them. As a result, bit 0 of the status does not recognise these latter three keys.

IPC 2 — open serial port 1
This command is seven bytes in length, being 2 0 ? ? ? ? 1 and signals to the 8049 that it should monitor serial port 1 for input, and set up in preparation for output.

IPC 3 — open serial port 2
This performs a similar action to that above, but on port 2, with the command 3 0 ? ? ? ? 1.

IPC 4 — close serial port 1
This is the reverse of function 2, and is 4 0 ? ? ? ? 1: it tells the 8049 to stop monitoring the serial port.

IPC 5 — close serial port 2
This is similar to function 4, and is 5 0 ? ? ? ? 1.

IPC 6, 7, 8 — read serial port 1, port 2, keyboard
These functions are impractical to call from user programs.

IPC 9 — keyboard direct read
This scans the keyboard matrix directly, and is used by the SuperBASIC KEYROW function. The command is 9 1 0 0 0 0 r 2 where 'r' is the row number, from 0 to 7. The byte read with the command will have bits set if the relevant key is held down, otherwise it will be reset. The keyboard matrix *appears* to the programmer to be the layout in **Figure 3.1**.

Note that this does scan the three keys that the other functions miss, and the 8049 puts their values into empty locations in the 8 × 8 matrix, even though they are physically elsewhere.

IPC 10 — initiate sound process
This is the longest command, consisting of 23 bytes, with parameters corresponding to those in the SuperBASIC BEEP command. The command is:

Data bits returned

	0	1	2	3	4	5	6	7
Row 7	SHFT	CTRL	ALT	X	V	/	N	,
Number 6	8	2	6	Q	E	0	T	U
5	9	W	I	TAB	R	-	Y	O
4	L	3	H	1	A	P	D	J
3	[	CAPS	K	S	F	=	G	;
2	]	Z	.	C	B	£	M	'
1	ENTR	←	↑	ESC	→	\	SPC	↓
0	F4	F1	5	F2	F3	F5	4	7

Figure 3.1:   Keyboard Matrix.

$A $10 $44 $44 $AA $66 [16 parameters] $01

The parameters are (in bytes):

pitch+1
pitch2+1
LSB of grad_x
MSB of grad_x
LSB of duration
MSB of duration
wrap+16*grad_y
fuzzy+16*random

The meaning of each parameter is explained in the QL User Guide.

IPC 11 — kill sound process
This is another seven-byte command, being $B 0 ? ? ? ? 1 which kills all sound dead, ie it's equivalent to the SuperBASIC command BEEP with no parameters.

IPC 12 — microdrive reduced sensitivity
This function would appear to have no effect at all!

IPC 13 — change baud rate
The baud rate can be changed with this function, but it should not be used as it does not tell the rest of the system about the change. You should use MT.BAUD, described in Chapter 5, instead.

IPC 14 — random number generator
This command is $E 0 ? ? ? ? 2 which returns a pseudo-random number. It is best to use only the lowest four bits though, as the highest bits tend to be zero most of the time. This is not a very good way of generating random numbers, and it's better either to read the system variable SV.RAND, or to generate your own with the floating point maths routines.

IPC 15 — test
This command makes the 8049 do some form of self test, and returns a byte parameter. Every time I have used it, I get 255, so presumably if you get something else then the processor is somehow faulty.

All of these commands share certain features and, in particular, no checks at all are made on their validity — if any are wrong, the whole machine is liable to crash. In addition, the whole IPC communications process is very slow (in relation to instruction times), and when scanning the keyboard you should choose your rows to minimise the number of scans. To help in this, the corresponding keys of the two joystick sockets are each on a single row.

CHAPTER 4
Input/Output

A good deal of QDOS is concerned with the many parts of the input/ output system, the means by which characters are read and written to the various I/O devices, such as the screen and microdrives. QDOS I/O is said to be 'device independent', which (in theory) means that programs can be written to read and write data without knowing (or caring) what exactly the devices used are, as they all seem the same to the program. (There are some exceptions to this, though — pipes and the serial ports are not quite the same as other I/O devices (see Chapter 5).) The whole I/O system is re-directable, which means that additional devices can be added to the system to supplement (or even replace) the standard ones. The supplementary devices can be either entirely RAM-based, or included with additional hardware in ROMs.

The routines to control the I/O system fall broadly into two sections — there is the I/O sub-system (or IOSS) which is used directly by the system calls, and the driver parts of the system which control what actions are taken by each device, to suit the requests made by the IOSS. The former section is fixed, but the latter can be added to, and re-defined, by other system calls.

QDOS I/O is based on channels, each having a unique 32-bit identifier, the 'channel ID'. The I/O system uses two main areas of RAM — there is the channel table, used for storing the details of all the channels, open or closed, and the common heap, which is used for storing various other information to do with each channel, and with each type of channel in some cases.

The channel table starts directly after the job table, and is three times as large as the job table (ie $3*((RAM-32768)/512+32)/4$), with a maximum of 360 channels — it gives 168 channels on the 128K machine. It follows a similar format to the job table, consisting of long words either pointing to a section in the common heap (known as the channel definition block), or containing $FF000000 if the channel is closed. The format of a channel ID is that the low word is a reference to the location in the channel table, and the high word is a tag that increments after each channel is opened. After a switch-on, there are normally three defined channels — $0 is the system channel, corresponding to the lower window (#0 from SuperBASIC), $00010001 corresponding to the PRINT window

33

(#1 from SuperBASIC), and $00020002 corresponding to the LIST window (#2). The former two channels should really not ever be closed, as they are used by the system for certain important output functions, covered later.

There are two main types of I/O devices — those based on storage media, which are directory-oriented, and the others, which are not directory-oriented. The former type are known as directory device drivers, while the latter are known as simple device drivers. On the standard QL system there is only one type of directory device driver, namely the micro-drive, all other devices being simple device drivers. Each type of device has a name, used for identifying the device and its parameters, if any. The name consists of a few characters defining the device's main type, and optionally may be followed by an underscore and then parameters. For directories, the main type name has to be followed by a drive number, eg MDV1_. Whether the channel names are upper or lower case is not important, so MDV1_NAME is identical to mdv1_name. The QL is regrettably non-standard in one important area — instead of using carriage return (CHR$ 13) for terminating records and lines, line-feed (CHR$ 10) is used instead, so beware if porting software between different 68000 series machines and the QL. The standard types of devices are:

Console I/O

This is the main screen device, used for printing characters and reading the keyboard. It has the general name CON, followed by various parameters defining the window size, position, and keyboard buffer, in the form:

CON_widXdepfAxorgXyorg_buffr

where 'wid' is the pixel width of the window (assuming a screen size of 512 × 256 with 0,0 at the top left), 'depf' the pixel depth of the window, 'xorg' and 'yorg' the position of the top left of the window, and 'buffr' the size of the type ahead keyboard buffer. When initially opened, the window colours are green ink on black paper (but these default colours get converted to black ink on black paper when the screen mode changes!). All pixel positions are made even, and if any or all of the parameters are omitted, the defaults are:

CON_448x180a32x16_128

Screen I/O

This is similar to the console device, but input from the keyboard is not allowed. Its general name is similar:

SCR_widxdepfAxorgXyorg

with the parameters having the same meanings as for CON. The defaults are also the same. SCR and CON channels have functions that are not available with other devices, for controlling such things as colour and graphics commands.

Serial ports

There are two serial ports on the QL, conforming to the RS232 protocol. Serial port 1 is configured as a data communication equipment (DCE) port, suitable for driving most serial printers, while port 2 is configured as a data terminal equipment (DTE) port, more suitable for accepting input from other devices. The difference between them is only in the way they are wired up — both ports are controlled by identical electronics. The actual control of the ports is handled by the 8049 IPC, which suffers from the disadvantage that both ports must have the same baud rate, and that this must be one of the standard rates. The general name is

SERnphz

with 'n' being the port number (1 or 2), 'p' being the parity (Even, Odd, Mark or Space), 'h' the handshaking (Ignore or Handshake), and 'z' the protocol — R for raw data with no EOF terminator, Z for control-Z (CHR\$ 26) being the EOF marker, and C the same as Z but with CR (CHR\$ 13) as the data separator instead of LF (CHR\$ 10). The standard serial drivers use buffers of 81 bytes in size on input and output. Only one channel may be open to each port at any one time — if any further attempts are made to open existing ports then the error 'in use' will occur. The default is SER1R.

Network I/O

The network protocol used on the QL is exclusive to Sinclair machines, and is known as QLNET. Up to 64 QLs and Spectrum/ZX Interface 1 combinations may be connected on a single net, each being given a 'station number' to distinguish them. Data is transferred between stations by two methods — either explicitly, with both the transmitting and receiving stations knowing the other's number, or by broadcasting, by using 'station 0'. With broadcasting, no handshaking is used, so if a station is not 'listening' to the net when another broadcasts, the data will be lost as the transmitter does not check for the usual acknowledgements. The general name is:

NETdirection_station

with 'direction' being 'I' for input, or 'O' for output (thus bi-directional channels are not allowed on the net), and 'station' being the number with which the calling station wishes to communicate. The default name is NETI_0.

Pipe I/O

A pipe is a section of memory set aside for a queue, and output data is put into the queue, and input read from the other end. This is the way that data passes between concurrent jobs, by one outputting data into the pipe, and the other inputting from it. Regrettably pipes are not quite the same as other I/O devices, and they are the reason for my saying QDOS was not quite device independent when it comes to I/O. The general name is

PIPE_length

with 'length' defining the length in bytes of the pipe to be created, or a length of 0 for an input pipe. Output pipes are handled just like any other output device, but input pipes are a little different — when opened, the channel ID of the existing pipe to be read must be passed in D3. For this reason, a job must open an output pipe before another job tries to open the corresponding input pipe. Pipes are only useful if multi-tasking, as when a pipe fills it will 'wait' for another job to read some bytes from it. Of course, if there is only one job then the data will never be read from the pipe, and the system will wait forever. The default is an input channel, namely

PIPE_0

Microdrive I/O

The microdrive is the only directory-based device in the standard QL, and is also the most complex. Microdrives consist of a continuous loop of tape, with data recorded in sectors of 512 bytes. As used on the Spectrum, they offer performance midway between slow cassettes and very fast disks, mainly because of the serial nature of the medium — if the sector you want has just passed the head, the entire tape has to be searched before you find it again, taking around seven seconds. Similar hardware is used in the QL drives as for the Spectrum, but the software is very different. The actual arrangement of data on the tape has been improved, to increase capacity, but the main difference is that sections of RAM known as 'slaving blocks' are used for storing copies of as many sectors as possible, so accessing the stored sectors is very much faster. A copy of the cartridge directory is also stored in RAM, so that when a file is opened the entire tape does not have to be searched to see if the file is already there. The QL does have to scan one sector on the tape when doing a directory, though, to make sure that the cartridge has not been changed since the directory was created. The general name is

MDVn_fname

where 'n' is the drive number (from 1–8) and 'fname' is the filename, of up to 36 characters. In theory, sub-directories could be supported, so that entering the BASIC command:

DIR mdvl_dir1_

could print up all the files starting with 'dir1_', such as mdv1_dir1_prog1 and mdv1_dir1_loader. Current versions of QDOS do not support this, but for Winchester support this sort of thing is rather necessary (else DIR win1_ could print up many hundreds of names), so it may be supported in later QDOS versions. Unfortunately there is no default for the micro-drive name or drive number, which have to be specified in full.

The actual mechanics behind each device are covered in the next chapter, but all I/O devices have to conform to certain specifications, using various linked lists which can be user-defined. There are two main linked lists for the I/O system — one for simple device drivers, and the other for directory device drivers. Each entry in the list, known as 'linkage blocks', stores the locations of the basic routines that control the device. For simple I/O drivers, the entry consists of four long words:

0	used by QDOS to form link to next entry
4	I/O routine
8	open routine
$C	close routine

For directory drivers, the entry consists of at least 10 long words, namely:

0	used by QDOS to form link to next entry
4	I/O routine
8	open routine
$C	close routine
$10	forced slaving routine
$14	reserved for Rename (not yet implemented)
$18	reserved for Truncate (not yet implemented)
$1C	format routine
$20	length of physical definition block (explained later)
$24	(word) length of drive name, followed by ASCII value of name

37

For the standard drivers, these linkage blocks lie in ROM, because the links never have to be altered, as the in-built drivers are always last in the list. For user-added drivers, in ROM or RAM, the blocks *must* be in RAM (normally the common heap) so that QDOS can put a suitable value in the link location. It's also important to note that directory devices must always have a drive number following their name, and that medium names must consist of a 16-bit random number (determined at the time of format) followed by 10 ASCII bytes. Drive numbers can range from 1 to 8 inclusive.

There is one such linkage block for each device driver in the system, and for directory device drivers there is also an area of RAM set aside for each drive, known as the 'physical definition block'. The block is allocated by the IOSS, using the size specified in the linkage block.

Channel definition block

When any channel is opened, a 'channel definition block' is allocated (again in the common heap), containing a certain minimum amount of information. Device drivers can define how big a definition block they need, but the usage of the first $14 bytes is determined by the IOSS, in this form:

$00	CH.LEN	long	length of this definition block
$04	CH.DRIVR	long	pointer to linkage block of device driver
$08	CH.OWNER	long	ID of owner job
$0C	CH.RFLAG	long	location to be set when space released
$10	CH.TAG	word	channel tag
$12	CH.STAT	byte	status: 0 OK, $FF A1 passed absolute, $80 A1 passed relative to A6; other negative values — waiting
$13	CH.ACTN	byte	action required for waiting job (value of D0)
$14	CH.JOBWT	long	ID of job waiting for I/O
$18	CH.END		drivers may use this area onwards

For directory drivers, channel definition blocks have a fixed length of $A0 bytes, and the rest of it is defined to be:

$18	FS.NEXT	long	link to next channel for this file system
$1C	FS.ACCESS	long	access mode defined when opened (in D3)
$1D	FS.DRIVE	byte	drive ID (from 0–15)
$1E	FS.FILNR	word	file number on drive
$20	FS.NBLOK	word	block number containing next byte
$22	FS.NBYTE	word	next byte from block
$24	FS.EBLOK	word	block number containing byte after EOF
$26	FS.EBYTE	word	byte after EOF
$28	FS.CBLOK	long	pointer to slave block table for current slave block
$2C	FS.UPDT	byte	set when file is updated

$32	FS.FNAME	2+36 bytes	filename
$58	FS.SPARE	72 bytes unused	
$A0	FS.END		end of block

Physical definition block

There is one of these in the common heap for every drive of a directory driver. Its beginning is similar to a channel definition block, and the IOSS defines the usage of the first $22 bytes:

$10	FS.DRIVR	long	pointer to driver
$14	FS.DRIVN	byte	drive number
$15		byte	reserved
$16	FS.MNAME	12 bytes	word followed by 10 bytes of ASCII of medium name
$22	FS.FILES	byte	number of files open

The length of a directory driver's definition block is defined by an entry in its linkage block.

Having covered the way the IOSS allocates channel and physical definition blocks, and the way device names are specified, let's now move on to the actual system calls for I/O. These are handled by trap #2, for the main allocation routines such as Open, and trap #3, for actual input and output, and file operations. The way the IOSS handles each call is described, but the way in which the individual devices react to the calls is covered in the next chapter.

I/O allocation routines

IO.OPEN — open a channel: TRAP #2 with D0=1

Entry:	D1.L	job ID (−1 for 'current job')
	D3.L	open type, 0–4 (pipe ID for input pipes)
	A0.L	address of channel name (word followed by ASCII)

Exit:	D1	job ID
	D2	preserved
	D3	preserved
	A0	new channel ID
	A1	preserved
	A2	preserved
	A3	preserved

Errors: −2   invalid job ID
            −3   out of memory
            −6   channel not opened — too many
            −7   file or device not found
            −8   file already exists
            −9   file or device in use
            −12   bad device name (eg parameters wrong)

Action: The value of D3 determines the type of the Open (except for pipes) — these are:

0   old exclusive device
1   old shared device
2   new exclusive device
3   new overwrite file
4   open directory

For simple I/O drivers, there is no difference between types 0–3 (and type 4 is not allowed), the types being intended for directory drivers. (In QDOS 1.03 and earlier, type 2 is not supported on microdrive files.) The device name must be in the usual QDOS string form, with a word defining the length of the string, followed by the ASCII of the string itself. If an error occurs during the Open operation, then the channel will not be allocated.

To start with, the IOSS searches for the first unused entry in the channel table, giving an error if there is no room in the table. The first Open routine in the device driver list is then called, and the error code is tested on return. If the error was 'not found', the next Open routine is called from the list, until the list is exhausted, when the directory device list is interrogated similarly until it too is exhausted, which gives an error return to the calling job. If any other error occurs, then a return is made to the job, otherwise the Open call must have been successful and further steps are taken. The returned location of the channel definition block is stored in the channel table, along with the linkage block location, the owner job, and the channel tag. Location CH.RFLAG is set to the highest byte of the long word in the channel table, so it is marked 'unused' when the area is reclaimed. Next CH.STAT, CH.ACTN and CH.JOBWT are all zeroed, and SV.CHMAX updated if required, and an exit made with no errors.

IO.CLOSE — close a channel: TRAP #2 with D0=2

Entry: A0.L   channel ID

Exit:	D1	preserved
	D2	preserved
	D3	preserved
	A0	corrupted
	A1	preserved
	A2	preserved
	A3	preserved

Errors:	−1	channel not open

Action: The specified channel is closed, and all common heap space allocated for it is normally reclaimed. Note that no other errors are expected by the system apart from 'channel not open'.

The appropriate linkage block is found, and the Close routine called. The only other action taken by the IOSS is for the appropriate channel table entry to have its high byte set to $FF, to mark it closed and ready for use by another channel. The actual Close routine in the device driver is responsible for releasing the common heap space, and this may not always occur at the time of closing, but may wait until, say, a buffer has been emptied.

IO.FORMT — format a medium: TRAP #2 with D0=3

Entry:	A0.L	pointer to medium name

Exit:	D1.W	number of good sectors
	D2.W	total number of sectors on media
	D3	preserved
	A0	corrupted
	A1	preserved
	A2	preserved
	A3	preserved

Errors:	−3	out of memory
	−7	device not found
	−9	device in use
	−14	format failed

Action: The specified medium is formatted and given the required name. The medium name should be stored in usual form, namely a word giving its length followed by the ASCII of the name, and should consist of the directory device name, drive number, followed by '_' then up to 10 bytes for the name. (The 'random' number also stored on the medium is handled by the Format routine in the driver.)

41

First each entry in the directory device list is checked until the drive name matches and the validity of the following drive number and underscore verified; an error return of 'device not found' is made if no matches or the drive number is invalid. Presuming the suitable definition block has been found, then the Format routine pointed from within the block is called, and an exit made to the calling job.

IO.DELET — delete a file: TRAP #2 with D0=4

Entry:	D1.L	job ID (or −1 for 'current job')
	A0.L	location of channel name

Exit:	D1	corrupted
	D2	preserved
	D3	corrupted
	A0	corrupted
	A1	corrupted
	A2	corrupted
	A3	preserved

Errors:	−3	out of memory
	−6	not deleted — too many channels open
	−7	file not found
	−12	bad device name

Action: The specified file is removed from the device, which must be a directory device.

Similar action is taken to IO.OPEN, with only the directory device list being scanned, but the IOSS sets D3 to $FF instead of the usual range of values.

Input/output routines

These all use TRAP #3, with generally similar parameters. In particular, most routines require a timeout, specified in D3.W. This has three ranges — if it is 0, then the action will be attempted within one frame (1/50th or 1/60th of a second), and a 'not complete' error generated if this was not sufficient time to complete the action. If the timeout is a positive number, then the I/O routine will have that number of frames to finish. A timeout of −1 indicates 'wait until completion'. The idea of a timeout is not just because some routines are 'slow', but is a result of the multi-tasking nature of QDOS. For example, suppose a channel is being used by a job for input from the CON_ device (ie the keyboard). If another job tries to output to the same channel, it must be prevented until the first job has finished with it, hence the need for timeouts. If the timeout specified by the second job expires before the first job relinquishes the channel, then the trap will return 'not complete', but if the timeout was long enough for the I/O to finish, then the second job will be able to output via the contended channel. Because of the way in which QDOS handles timeouts, it is very important that when in supervisor mode all I/O timeouts *must* be zero, and if the error 'not complete' occurs then repeat the call, again with a timeout of zero.

The channel ID is always passed in A0.L, and is never modified by the trap. D3 is also never modified. All trap #3s take similar action, because it is the responsibility of the device driver to differentiate between the different functions, which fall into three categories — simple I/O, screen I/O, and file I/O. The action taken by the IOSS for all the traps is as follows.

First the channel ID is checked to see it is valid, then CH.STAT examined — if CH.STAT has bit 7 set then a job is already waiting for the I/O, so the scheduler is entered unless the timeout is 0, in which case an error return 'not complete' is made. If a job is not waiting for the channel, then bit 7 of CH.STAT is set, to show that the calling job is about to wait for it, then the value of D0 is tested. D0 is used to indicate the I/O action required and, for actions that require strings of bytes to be read or written, D1 is zeroed for later use. The value of D0 is stored in CH.ACTN, for use by the device I/O routine, which is then called. On return, the error code is tested — if the action was 'not complete' then the timeout is tested, and if the timeout has expired then an error return is made. Otherwise CH.STAT is made negative and the location of CH.STAT stored in JB.HOLD of the calling job, so that it's cleared when the I/O action is complete, the timeout stored in JB.STAT, and JB.PRIOR zeroed. Finally control passes into the scheduler to re-schedule the jobs, as the current job has to wait for the I/O operation. If the error after calling the device routine was not 'not complete', then the routine returns to the calling job with the error code (or 0 if there were no errors) after clearing CH.STAT. The action the scheduler takes with waiting I/O is covered in detail later in Chapter 6.

One problem with QDOS I/O is that the Break combination of keys never gets tested, hence the lack of a 'break' error message. Thus if you try to do an I/O operation with an infinite timeout and the operation never finishes, the machine will just hang. This is a particularly common problem with net and pipe operations, though there is one exception — any I/O traps called from job 0 (SuperBASIC) can be interrupted by pressing CTRL SPACE, and will give the error 'not complete'. This is a result of a piece of code in the keyboard scan routine, explained in Chapter 6.

Simple I/O traps

All I/O errors can potentially return any error, depending on the device driver. In particular, drivers added to the system can generate their own special error messages, though TST.L D0 will still give NE if any error has occurred. The expected error messages are covered after each trap.

All TRAP #3s are handled in an identical manner by the IOSS, the device drivers being responsible for differing actions to be taken. Firstly the IOSS logically ANDs D0 with $7F, so that D0 may be set up with a byte-sized instruction. Next the channel ID is examined and the appropriate entry checked to ensure that the channel is indeed open, and if it is then the tag value for the channel is compared to the high word of the channel ID to make doubly sure that the channel ID is valid. Following this, the CH.STAT has bit 7 tested to see if the channel is already 'busy' — if it is, then either a 'not complete' error is returned (if the timeout has expired) or the scheduler is entered. The operation code (in D0) is stored in CH.ACTN, so that the driver knows what it has to do, and the I/O routine, calculated from CH.DRIVR, called to do the operation. On return, D0 is tested to see if a 'not complete' error has occurred, and as long as it is not (or the timeout was 0) then the registers are restored, CH.STAT zeroed, and the trap will exit. If the error was 'not complete', then the calling job's ID is stored in CH.ACTN, and the location of CH.STAT stored in JB.HOLD (so that it will be cleared when the job is released), and the current value of the timeout is stored in JB.STAT as a delay time. Next JB.PRIOR is zeroed, to make sure the job does not start until the I/O is finished, and a return made via the scheduler. The I/O operation will be re-attempted under interrupts by a task in the scheduler linked list, until it either times out or completes.

The IOSS makes no checks at all on the validity of D0 on entry, so that additional features can be added via the individual device drivers. Note that certain unused values of D0 are reserved for future enhancements.

IO.PEND — test for pending input: TRAP #3 with D0=0

Entry:	D3.W	timeout
	A0.L	channel ID

Exit:	D1	corrupted
	D2	preserved
	D3	preserved
	A0	preserved
	A1	corrupted
	A2	preserved
	A3	preserved

Errors:	−1	no pending input
	−6	invalid channel ID
	−10	end of file

Action: The input status of the channel is read from the device. An 'error' value of 0 in D0 signals that there is data waiting to be read.

IO.FBYTE — fetch a byte from a channel : TRAP #3 with D0=1

Entry:	D3.W	timeout
	A0.L	channel ID

Exit:	D1.B	byte read
	D2	preserved
	D3	preserved
	A0	preserved
	A1	corrupted
	A2	preserved
	A3	preserved

Errors:	−1	not complete
	−6	invalid channel ID
	−10	end of file (ie no more bytes to read)

Action: An attempt is made to read a byte from the channel within the specified timeout.

IO.FLINE — fetch a line of bytes ending in LF: TRAP #3 with D0=2

Entry:	D2.W	buffer size (in bytes)
	D3.W	timeout
	A0.L	channel ID
	A1.L	start address of buffer

Exit:	D1.W	number of bytes returned
	D2	preserved
	D3	preserved
	A0	preserved
	A1	pointer to one past the last character
	A2	preserved
	A3	preserved

Errors: −1   not complete
             −5   buffer overflow (ie too many characters read)
             −6   invalid channel ID
             −10   end of file

Action: A sequence of bytes is read from the channel terminating in an LF character. The character count includes the LF byte, which is stored at the end of the buffer (at −1(A1) on return).

When using this for a CON channel, the cursor is first enabled. Each key pressed is echoed in the window, the left and right cursor keys work in the usual way, and in conjunction with CTRL they delete characters. Other non-numeric characters are ignored; Break will only work with software running as job 0, and will give a 'not complete' error. If no error occurs, the cursor is disabled when finished.

IO.FSTRG — fetch a string of bytes: TRAP #3 with D0=3

Entry: D2.W   buffer size (in bytes)
            D3.W   timeout
            A0.L   channel ID
            A1.L   location of start of buffer

Exit: D1.W   number of bytes read
            D2   preserved
            D3   preserved
            A0   preserved
            A1   updated pointer
            A2   preserved
            A3   preserved

Errors: −1   not complete
            −6   invalid channel ID
            −10   end of file

Action: The specified number of bytes is read from the channel and stored in the buffer. (Buffer overflow cannot occur as the trap will only attempt to read a maximum of D2 bytes.) It is much more efficient to read files using this trap, compared with repeatedly calling IO.FBYTE. For CON channels, the keys pressed are *not* echoed in the window.

Channels opened as directories should be read using the trap, with D2 set to 64 each time. The trap will then read each header, in the form covered in the File I/O section later in this chapter, until an EOF occurs.

46

IO.EDLIN — edit a line of characters: TRAP #3 with D0=4

Entry: D1   high word: cursor position
            D1   low word: current line length
            D2.W   size of buffer (in bytes)
            D3.W   timeout
            A0.L   channel ID
            A1.L   pointer to character at current cursor position

Exit: D1.W   line length (including terminator)
            D2   preserved
            D3   preserved
            A0   preserved
            A1   pointer to byte past end of line
            A2   preserved
            A3   preserved

Errors: −1   not complete
            −5   buffer overflow
            −6   invalid channel ID

Action: With the standard QL, this trap will produce the error 'bad parameter' if the channel is not CON type. This is potentially a very useful trap, but is tricky to use. To edit a line, you should print it out yourself, using any of the following traps, then position the cursor where you want it. When this trap is issued, nothing is printed except for a flashing cursor. The edit can be ended by pressing cursor up, cursor down, or ENTER. The count includes the terminating character, which itself is stored at the end of the buffer (at −1(A1)). On return, there is no way of finding out exactly where the cursor was when the edit was terminated.

IO.SBYTE — send a byte to the channel: TRAP #3 with D0=5

Entry: D1.B   byte to be sent
            D3.W   timeout

Exit: D1   corrupted
            D2   preserved
            D3   preserved
            A0   preserved
            A1   corrupted
            A2   preserved
            A3   preserved

Errors:	−1	not complete
	−6	invalid channel ID
	−11	drive full

Action: An attempt is made to send the byte to the channel within the given timeout.

IO.SSTRG — send a sequence of bytes: TRAP #3 with D0=7

Entry:	D2.W	number of bytes to send
	D3.W	timeout
	A0.L	channel ID
	A1.L	location of first byte to be sent

Exit:	D1.W	number of bytes sent in given time
	D2	preserved
	D3	preserved
	A0	preserved
	A1	points to 1 past last byte sent
	A2	preserved
	A3	preserved

Errors:	−1	not complete
	−6	invalid channel ID
	−11	drive full

Action: The sequence of bytes starting at (A1) is sent to the channel, and as many bytes as possible are sent in the allocated time. This is generally more efficient than repeatedly calling IO.SBYTE.

File I/O

There are several traps to deal with files, and note that most require the timeout to be infinite (ie −1) to work. Thus these traps are *not generally atomic* and cannot be called from supervisor mode. Certain file operations cannot normally be done on non-directory drivers, resulting in a 'bad parameter' error.

FS.POSAB — position absolute file pointer: TRAP #3 with D0=$42

Entry:	D1.L	file position required
	D3.W	timeout
	A0.L	channel ID

Exit:	D1	new file position
	D2	preserved
	D3	preserved
	A0	preserved
	A1	corrupted
	A2	preserved
	A3	preserved

Errors:	−1	not complete
	−6	invalid channel ID
	−10	end of file

Action: The pointer to the file is positioned as per the value of D1, if possible. If this is past the end of the file, then the pointer will be set to the last byte of the file.

FS.POSRE — position file pointer relatively: TRAP #3 with D0=$43

Entry:	D1.L	signed relative pointer offset
	D3.W	timeout
	A0.L	channel ID

Exit:	D1.L	new file position
	D2	preserved
	D3	preserved
	A0	preserved
	A1	corrupted
	A2	preserved
	A3	preserved

Errors:	−1	not complete
	−6	invalid channel ID
	−10	end of file

Action: This moves the file pointer as per the signed value of D1. If the resulting value is less than 0 or greater than the file length, then it will be set to one or the other. A value of 0 is useful for reading the current position.

FS.MDINF — read medium information: TRAP #3 with D0=$45

Entry:	D3.W	timeout

	A0.L	channel ID
	A1.L	location of buffer for medium name

Exit:	D1 high word	unused sectors
	D1 low word	good sectors
	D2	preserved
	D3	preserved
	A0	preserved
	A1	1 byte past end of medium name
	A2	corrupted
	A3	corrupted

Errors:	−1	not complete
	−6	invalid channel ID

Action: The 10-byte medium name is read into the buffer, and the sector details put into D1. A sector is defined to be 512 bytes, regardless of the actual sector size of the media.

File headers

Every file has a header which is hidden from the normal I/O operations. It is either 64 bytes long for directory drivers, or 15 bytes long for other device drivers. The first byte of non-directory headers is always fixed to $FF, and 'invisible' to calling software. The format of both headers is:

00	long	file length
04	byte	file access: currently always 0
05	byte	file type: 0 except for EXECable files when it's 1
06	long	size of data space for EXECable files
$0A	long	unused

For directory drivers only, there is additionally:

$0E	word	length of filename
$10	36 bytes for filename	
$34	long	date of update (not yet implemented)
$38	long	reference date (not yet implemented)
$3A	long	date of backup (not yet implemented)

FS.HEADS — set file header: TRAP #3 with D0=$46

Entry: D3.W   timeout

	A0.L	channel ID
	A1.L	start of header
Exit:	D1.W	length of set header
	D2	preserved
	D3	preserved
	A0	preserved
	A1	corrupted
	A2	preserved
	A3	preserved
Errors:	−1	not complete
	−6	invalid channel ID

Action: The header is set for the defined channel. For non-device drivers this will be 15, and the MDV driver returns 14. (This means that you cannot set the unused three words for date information, and also not rename the file with this trap.)

FS.HEADR — read file header: TRAP #3 with D0=$47

Entry:	D2.W	buffer length
	D3.W	timeout
	A0.L	channel ID
	A1.L	location of buffer for header
Exit:	D1.W	size of header read
	D2	preserved
	D3	preserved
	A0	preserved
	A1	1 past end of buffer read
	A2	preserved
	A3	preserved
Errors:	−1	not complete
	−5	buffer overflow
	−6	invalid channel ID

Action: The channel has its header read into the buffer, provided that the buffer is large enough. It is particularly useful for knowing how much space to allocate for files about to be loaded.

FS.LOAD — load bytes from device: TRAP #3 with D0=$48

Entry:	D2.L	number of bytes required
	D3.W	timeout (should always be −1)
	A0.L	channel ID
	A1.L	location for bytes to be loaded (must be even)

Exit:	D1	corrupted
	D2	preserved
	D3	preserved
	A0	preserved
	A1	1 past location of last byte
	A2	preserved
	A3	preserved

Errors:	−1	not complete
	−6	invalid channel ID
	−10	end of file

Action: An attempt is made to load the specified number of bytes from the channel. It is recommended that the timeout is always −1 to ensure successful operation. Note that this is not necessarily similar to IO.FSTRG, as the bytes may be loaded by this call in a 'random access' fashion for speed, instead of the serial operation of the former.

FS.SAVE — save bytes of memory: TRAP #3 with D0=$49

Entry:	D2.L	number of bytes to save
	D3.W	timeout (should be −1)
	A0.L	channel ID
	A1.L	start address of save (must be even)

Exit:	D1	corrupted
	D2	preserved
	D3	preserved
	A0	preserved
	A1	1 past location of last byte saved
	A2	preserved
	A3	preserved

Errors:	−1	not complete
	−6	invalid channel ID
	−11	drive full

Action: The bytes are saved on to the channel, and a timeout of −1 is recommended for successful operation.

FS.CHECK — check for pending operations: TRAP #3 with D0=$40

Entry:	D3.W	timeout
	A0.L	channel ID

Exit:	D1	corrupted
	D2	preserved
	D3	preserved
	A0	preserved
	A1	corrupted
	A2	preserved
	A3	preserved

Errors:	−1	not complete
	−6	invalid channel ID

Action: This trap allows testing of any pending operations on a file. Generally buffering occurs on all file I/O, and this allows a program to see if all pending operations have actually finished or not.

FS.FLUSH — flush buffers of a file: TRAP #3 with D0=$41

Entry:	D3.W	timeout
	A0.L	channel

Exit:	D1	corrupted
	D2	preserved
	D3	preserved
	A0	preserved
	A1	corrupted
	A2	preserved
	A3	preserved

Errors:	−1	not complete
	−6	invalid channel ID

Action: This makes sure that all output buffers used by the channel are physically written out from any internal buffers. This is particularly useful for ensuring that a file is complete, before doing something drastic such as a complete system reset.

CHAPTER 5
Device Drivers

The QL contains various device drivers within QDOS, designed in such a way that they can be altered and added to with additional drivers. This chapter covers the workings of each device on the standard QL.

Simple I/O

To save repetition, QDOS has a standard way of handling simple serial devices. The method is used by the inbuilt device drivers SER, NET and PIPE, and can also be used by additional drivers. It requires only three routines to be specific to the driver, apart from the Open and Close routines — test for pending input, input a byte, and output a byte. Given these, the IOSS looks after the other QDOS features, in these ways:

IO.FLINE: Fetch a line of bytes: the 'fetch byte' routine is called until either an error occurs, the buffer length is extended, or an LF character is received.

IO.FSTRG: Fetch a string of bytes: the 'fetch byte' routine is called until either an error occurs, or the buffer length is exceeded.

IO.EDLIN: Edit a line: not implemented, and produces a 'bad parameter' error.

IO.SSTRG: Send a string of bytes: each byte in the buffer is sent via the output routine, until either all the bytes have been sent, or any error has occurred.

FS.HEADS: Set file header: this sends 15 bytes of header via the 'output byte' routine, consisting of $FF followed by the 14 bytes of the header. A premature exit is made if an error occurs.

FS.HEADR: Read file header: first a single byte is read and compared with $FF, and if it is not $FF then a 'bad parameter' error return will be made. If it was, then 14 further bytes are read, unless any error occurs.

FS.LOAD: Load a file: the routine IO.FSTRG is used to read the bytes.

FS.SAVE: Save a file: the routine IO.SSTRG is used to output the bytes.

QDOS functions used by trap #3 with D0 from $8 to $45 inclusive all give the 'bad parameter' error with devices that use this simple I/O driver.

Queue handling

There is a standard way for queues to be implemented via QDOS. This is based on a header of at least 18 bytes, in the form of four long words. The OS uses bit 31 of the first word, but the rest is left alone and can be used by user device drivers. The second word points to the end of the queue, the third points to the physical end of the queue (ie the next location to store a byte), and the fourth points to the front of the queue (ie the next location for a byte to be read from). After the fourth word comes the queue itself.

Device SER — the serial ports

This is the simplest of the inbuilt device drivers, mainly using the standard routines of QDOS. The actual handling of bytes is done during interrupts via the IPC, with the driver only concerned with controlling the input and output queues. Its channel definition block is created in the following form (the first $18 bytes conform to the IOSS requirements covered previously):

$18	SER.CHNO	byte	port number, 1 or 2
$1A	SER.PAR	byte	parity: 0 none, 1 odd, 2 even, 3 mark, 4 space
$1C	SER.TXHS	byte	transmit handshake flag: $FF ignore, 0 handshake
$1E	SER.PROT	byte	protocol flag: $FF for R, 0 for Z, 1 for C
$20	SER.RXQ		receive queue header followed by queue
$82	SER.TXQ		transmit queue header followed by queue
$E4	SER.END		end of definition block

Open routine: After checking the parameters of the device name, interrupts are disabled and the appropriate system variable (SV.SER1C/SER2C) tested to see if there is already a receive channel in existence. If there is, then it is tested to see if it has been emptied — if not then it means that a channel is already open to the serial port, so the error return 'in use' is made. Otherwise, space is claimed in the common heap for the definition block of size $E4 bytes. Next both the receive and transmit queues are set up, each 81 bytes in length, and the receive queue address stored in the appropriate system variable. Next the system sets up the necessary flags in the definition block, and then tells the IPC to open an RS232 channel on the serial port, before enabling interrupts and returning.

Close routine: First the IPC is told to close its serial port, then the transmit queue is set to empty.

For general I/O, the simple serial handler is used, based very much on the standard queue handling routines with a few modifications. The 'send a byte' converts an LF into a CR (so long as option R is not selected), then bit 7 of the byte is adjusted if necessary to suit the parity type chosen, and the byte put into the transmit queue. The 'receive byte' routine starts by reading a byte from the receive queue, and the parity of the byte is checked. If the check fails, the error return 'transmit error' will occur, then any CRs are converted to LFs (unless Raw option is selected). The 'test pending' routine uses the equivalent queue routine to test the receive queue status. Note that, due to the way the interrupt routine works, no actual I/O of bytes occurs on the serial ports while in supervisor mode.

Current versions of the QL suffer problems when using the serial ports for input. In particular, baud rates greater than 1200 are unreliable, and all input regardless of speed should be done using IO.FSTR or preferably FS.LOAD to avoid data corruption. The baud rate is set by this trap:

MT.BAUD — set the baud rate: TRAP #1 with D0=$12

Entry:	D1.W	baud rate

Exit:	D1	corrupted
	D2	preserved
	D3	preserved
	A0	preserved
	A1	preserved
	A2	preserved
	A3	preserved

Errors:	−15	bad parameter (as rate not recognised)

Action: The serial ports baud rate is set according to the value of D1, which can only be either 75, 300, 600, 1200, 2400, 4800, 9600 or 19200.

First a table of valid baud rates is searched for the correct value, and (if found) a rate number is calculated, which is 7 for 75 baud, down to 0 for 19200 baud. The contents of SV.TIMOV is calculated to be INT(1200/baud)+1, to be used as a crude timer during transmit interrupts, and the current contents of SV.TMOD has the rate number ORed into its lowest three bits. The new value of TMOD is then sent to the IPC via command $0D, interrupts re-enabled, and a return is made.

Device NET — the network

The network used in the QL and the ZX Spectrum is a simple two-wire connection, allowing up to 64 machines to be interconnected. Data is sent over the net in 'packets' of 255 bytes of data. Before explaining the format, it is useful to examine the channel definition block format:

$18	NET.HEDR	byte	destination station number (equivalent to NCIRIS on the Spectrum)
$19	NET.SELF	byte	this station number
$1A	NET.BLKL	byte	LSB of data block number
$1B	NET.BLKH	byte	MSB of data block number (these are in reverse order because of the way words are stored for the Z80 on the Spectrum)
$1C	NET.TYPE	byte	packet type: 0 data, 1 EOF packet
$1D	NET.NBYT	byte	number of bytes in data block
$1E	NET.DCHK	byte	data checksum
$1F	NET.HCHK	byte	header checksum
$20	NET.DATA	255 bytes	data block
$11F	NET.RPNT	byte	pointer to current position in data block
$120	NET.END		end of channel definition block

The protocol acts in the following way. The sender listens to the network to wait until it isn't being used by anyone else, and when the network is free the sender transmits the eight bytes of header, from NET.HDR to NET.HCHK inclusive down the cable serially at a high rate. Unless the sender is broadcasting (ie sending to any listening machines), it tests to see if the receiving station transmits a byte of acknowledgement, in the form of its station number. If the byte is not received or does not correspond to the desired receiver, then the sender repeats the whole process until successful or until it times out. If the sender was broadcasting, no checks are made on the acknowledgement. Next the data packet is sent (which may not necessarily be the full 255 bytes) and another acknowledgement tested for (unless broadcasting) — if it is not found then the whole process is re-tried. Network channels are single direction channels, the direction determined by the name, though any number of channels of input or output can be open at once.

Open routine: After checking the parameters in the name, $120 bytes are claimed from the common heap for the channel definition. The host station number is then copied from SV.NETNR to NET.SELF, the destination copied from the device specifier to NET.DEST, NET.TYPE set to suit the direction, and a return made.

Close routine: If the channel is set for output, then NET.TYPE is set to show 'EOF packet', and NET.RPNT copied to NET.NBYT. The routine then waits for any microdrives that are turning to stop, so that the timing will not be upset by them. The packet will then try to be sent, but if the attempt fails then it will be tried a further 1399 times, when the QL will give up (though the calling job will not know it was unsuccessful, as the routine does not cause an error return). If the transmission was successful (or unsuccessful 1400 times), the routine finishes by reclaiming the channel definition area from the common heap. If the channel was an input channel, the only action taken is for the definition block to be reclaimed.

For general I/O, the simple serial handler is used as follows. The 'pending input' tests to see if the channel is an output channel, and if it is then the error return 'bad parameter' is made. If the buffer is empty, then an attempt is made to read a packet from the net, and the process repeats if successful. If the buffer is not empty, then NET.RPNT is compared with NET.NBYT, and an 'EOF' return made if there are no more bytes to be read from the buffer and it was an 'EOF' buffer. For the 'receive a byte' routine, the 'pending input' routine is called and, if there was no error, the appropriate byte is read from the buffer and NET.RPNT incremented. The 'send byte' routine checks that the channel is an output channel (otherwise 'bad parameter' occurs), and if so then NET.RPNT is incremented. If NET.RPNT reaches 256 (ie there is no room in the buffer) then the byte's value is saved, NET.TYPE is set to $FF, the packet is transmitted, and the byte value restored. In either case, the byte is placed in the appropriate position within the buffer, and then NET.RPNT updated.

There is no trap to set the QL's station number, and this is done simply by writing a byte of suitable value into SV.NETNR at $28037, between 1 and 64 inclusive.

Device PIPE — internal pipes

Pipes are queues maintained in memory, for communication between jobs. They differ from other queues in that they are addressed in a similar way to any other I/O device, though with the difference that when opening an input pipe the channel ID of the corresponding output pipe has to be passed into D3. The channel definition block is in the following form:

$18	CH.QIN	pointer to input queue (0 if output pipe)
$1C	CH.QOUT	pointer to output queue (0 if input pipe)
$20	CH.QEND	end of definition (input) or queue header followed by queue (output)

The input and output queues conform to the standard QDOS form, and are handled by the general queue routines.

Open routine: If a size is specified in the device name (ie it is to be an output pipe) then space is made of $31+pipe size in the common heap, and the output queue header is initialised to 'empty'. Opening an input queue is rather more complex, as the corresponding input queue had to be found and linked into the channel definition block, and this is done in the following way. Given the output channel ID, the corresponding definition block is found and checked to see if it is indeed a pipe, with 'bad parameter' occurring if not. Next, a channel definition block of $20 bytes is claimed in the common heap, and the location of the input channel's definition block stored in the output channel's CH.QEND word. Finally the location of the output queue is stored in CH.QIN of the input channel.

Close routine: Closing a pipe is rather different depending on its direction (input or output), as problems can occur with jobs otherwise. For example, suppose one job opens an output pipe, sends its data to it and then closes it. The system should not remove the queue from memory when it is closed, but should wait until the job that is reading from the pipe has read all the data, otherwise the data would be lost. When closing an input pipe, the heap space is reclaimed after noting the location of the corresponding queue. The contents of CH.END are then examined, and if negative (ie the output channel has finished with the queue, too) then it is reclaimed, else it is zeroed to show that the receiving job has finished with the queue and is not reclaimed. When closing an input channel, the definition block is reclaimed if CH.END is zero (ie the inputting job has finished with it), otherwise it is made negative to show that the sending job has finished with it.

General I/O with pipes is based on the standard queue drivers in conjunction with the simple serial I/O routines, though checks are made to ensure that the pipe is of the right direction (ie input or output).

Devices SCR and CON — the screen and keyboard

To the device driver these two device types are the same, though SCR channels are marked to prevent attempts to read data from them. Output traps can do various things, including handling graphics and colour, but also the very important business of printing characters on the screen. Input from the CON device is via the keyboard, which may or may not be echoed on the screen, depending on the trap used. As the QL screen is composed of a large amount of memory, and the device drivers have to cope with windows, colours and stipples, as well as two different screen modes, the drivers are unfortunately rather slow when it comes to character output. However, the graphics routines are not, and they are very fast at doing complicated things like plotting, drawing lines and ellipses , and filling simultaneously. The format of the channel definition block is as follows:

$18	SD.XMIN	word	top lefthand position of window
$1A	SD.YMIN	word	
$1C	SD.XSIZE	word	window size

$1E	SD.YSIZE	word	
$20	SD.BORWD	word	border width
$22	SD.XPOS	word	current cursor position within window
$24	SD.YPOS	word	
$26	SD.XINC	word	cursor size
$28	SD.YINC	word	
$2A	SD.FOUNT	2 long	address of character fonts
$32	SD.SCRB	long	start of screen memory (always $20000)
$36	SD.PMASK	long	paper colour mask
$3A	SD.SMASK	long	strip colour mask
$3E	SD.IMASK	long	ink colour mask
$42	SD.CATTR	byte	character attributes:
			bit 0 — underline
			bit 1 — flash (mode 8 only)
			bit 2 — transparent background
			bit 3 — XOR
			bit 4 — double height
			bit 5 — extended width
			bit 6 — double width (or mode 8)
			bit 7 — graphics positioned characters
$43	SD.CURF	byte	cursor status: 0 suppressed, >0 visible
$44	SD.PCOLR	byte	paper colour byte
$45	SD.SCOLR	byte	strip colour byte
$46	SD.ICOLR	byte	ink colour byte
$47	SD.BCOLR	byte	border colour byte
$48	SD.NLSTA	byte	newline status: 0 none pending, 1 pending
$49	SD.FMOD	byte	fill mode: 0 off, 1 on
$4A	SD.YORG	f.p.	graphics window origin
$50	SD.XORG	f.p.	
$56	SD.SCAL	f.p.	scale factor for graphics
$5C	SD.FBUF	long	location of fill buffer
$60	SD.FUSE	long	pointer to user-defined fill vectors
$64	SD.KBD	long	0 (SCR) or start of keyboard queue header
$68	SD.END		end of SCR definition block (not CON)

All positions are defined on a pixel basis, assuming a constant screen size of 512×256. The variables marked 'f.p.' are stored in floating point format, which consists of six bytes, explained in a moment. For SCR channels, the definition block is $68 bytes long, but for CON channels it is $76+keyboard queue length. Each screen channel can have its own cursor, but there can only be one cursor active at a time. Switching between cursors in different screens may be accomplished by pressing CTRL C (though this character may be changed, being held in SV.CQCH). Either channel type has what are known as 'pending newlines', which has the result that a newline may not actually be issued when expected. For example, if printing is on the last line in a window, and an LF character is sent, the screen will *not* scroll up immediately, as the newline will be held 'pending'. Should any more characters be sent or certain other operations done, as detailed individually, then the screen will be scrolled, and the newline status set to 'not pending'.

61

Open routine: After checking the parameters, a suitably sized channel definition block is claimed from the heap, and certain variables initialised to these values:

SD.XINC	6 (mode 4) or 12 (mode 8)
SD.YINC	10
SD.SCAL	100
SD.CATTR	0 (mode 4) or $40 (mode 8)
SD.SCRB	$20000

Both fonts are initialised to values dependent on the ROM, the ink colour set to green, paper to black and no border. After this, the parameters defining the window's size and position are configured, and if an error occurs (eg the window will not fit on the screen) then the whole area is reclaimed from the heap, and an error return made. For CON devices, the keyboard queue header is set up to show 'empty' and linked into the keyboard queue list, and also put into SV.KEYQ as the current queue if another queue is not already defined as such.

Close routine: If the channel was a CON type, the keyboard queue is removed from the list of queues, and SV.KEYQ zeroed if it was the only one, otherwise it is updated to the next keyboard queue in the list. Finally the definition area is reclaimed from the common heap.

Input from CON channels use the keyboard, and all the possible combinations are shown in Appendix E. General I/O uses various routines, after checking to prevent input from an SCR device (which gives 'bad parameter'), as follows.

'Pending input', 'fetch byte' and 'fetch a string of bytes' all use the standard queue handling routines acting on the appropriate keyboard queue. Note that the characters are not echoed on the screen with the 'fetch' routines.

'Send a byte' and 'send a string of bytes' print the character pattern in the next position on the screen, with special action being taken for LFs. No error can occur with these routines except 'not complete' if the channel is already being used by another job for input, or if CTRL F5 has been pressed.

The special routines for CON devices are the 'fetch a line' and 'edit a line' traps. These are handled in an identical manner, though for 'fetch a line' the driver zeroes D1 first (the cursor position) and sets A1 to A0. The arrow keys move the cursor within the line, and delete single characters in either direction when used with CTRL. For the 'fetch line' trap, the only terminator is ENTER, but 'edit line' also allows the cursor up and down keys to terminate the edit. In QDOS versions 1.03 and earlier there is a slight bug in that, in the event of an error, such as 'buffer overflow', the cursor is not disabled as it normally is, and this can cause problems. These can be overcome simply by disabling the cursor after doing the trap. Note that this trap filters out certain keypresses, including all combinations with the function keys and the ALT key.

File I/O: Neither of the screen devices permit any of the file handling functions, and attempts to do so will produce the error return 'bad parameter'.

The screen drivers are unique among the standard devices as they support nearly 50 extra system calls to control graphics. It is possible that extra screen drivers may be available at a later date but, while the parameters will be the same as those specified shortly, the actions taken may not. The extra functions use TRAP #3 with D0 ranging in value from 9 to $36, and share similar attributes to the other trap #3 calls, particularly regarding channel IDs and timeouts.

Screen I/O functions

SD.EXTOP — perform external operation: TRAP #3 with D0=9

Entry: D1   parameter
          D2   parameter
          D3.W   timeout
          A0.L   channel ID
          A1   parameter
          A2.L   starting address of operation

Exit: D1   returned parameter
          D2   preserved
          D3   preserved
          A0   preserved
          A1   returned parameter
          A2   preserved

Errors: −1   not complete
          −6   invalid channel ID
          may be other types of errors, depending on routine

Action: This allows additional functions to be added to the screen drivers, by calling routine (A2). The values of the registers on entry are the usual ones set by the IOSS, but in particular A0 contains the start of the channel definition block. Three parameters can be passed to your routine and two

63

returned from it, in the registers shown. The routine may generate its own types of error.

One useful feature that can be done with this trap is to change the character height from the usual 10 or 20 pixels to 9. This allows 10% more lines to be fitted into any window, with only a small loss in clarity. This can be done with these lines:

```
              LEA CONEXT(PC),A2
              MOVE.L #CHANID,A0
              MOVEQ #9,D0          for external operation
              MOVEQ #-1,D3         timeout
              TRAP #3             do it
              RTS
CONEXT        MOVE.W #9,$28(A0)    set SD.YINC
              MOVEQ #0,D0          no error
              RTS
```

The new height will remain until changed when either an SD.SETSZ trap is issued, or when the screen mode is changed.

SD.PXENQ — read window size and cursor position in pixels: TRAP #3 with D0=$0A

Entry:	D3.W	timeout
	A0.L	channel ID
	A1.L	start of buffer for results

Exit:	D1	preserved
	D2	preserved
	D3	preserved
	A0	preserved
	A1	corrupted
	A2	preserved

Errors:	−1	not complete
	−6	invalid channel ID

Action: The window size and current cursor position in pixels (relative to the top left corner) are put in the buffer pointed to by A1, in this form:

0(A1)	window width
2(A1)	window depth
4(A1)	cursor x position

6(A1)   cursor y position
(all word sized)

First any pending newlines are activated, then the parameters copied directly from SD.XSIZE, SD.YSIZE, SD.XPOS and SD.YPOS into the buffer. In current versions of QDOS A1 is not corrupted, but this is not guaranteed in subsequent versions.

SD.CHENQ — read window size and cursor position in characters: TRAP #3 with D0=$0B

Entry:	D3.W	timeout
	A0.L	channel ID
	A1.L	start of buffer for results

Exit:	D1	preserved
	D2	preserved
	D3	preserved
	A0	preserved
	A1	corrupted
	A2	preserved

| *Errors:* | −1 | not complete |
| | −6 | invalid channel ID |

Action: The window size and cursor position are read, converted to character coordinates, and put in the buffer in the same form as the previous trap.

The SD.PXENQ routine is called, and then each parameter divided by the cursor width or height, as appropriate.

SD.BORDR — set border colour and width: TRAP #3 with D0=$0C

Entry:	D1.B	colour
	D2.W	width
	D3.W	timeout
	A0.L	channel ID

Exit:	D1	corrupted
	D2	preserved
	D3	preserved
	A0	preserved
	A1	preserved
	A2	preserved

Errors: −1   not complete
          −4   out of range (ie border will not fit in window)
          −6   invalid channel ID

Action: A border is put around the specified window, of the specified width and colour. A colour of $80 defines a transparent border, and if the border width is changed the cursor will be set to the top left position.

The colour byte is stored in SD.BCOLR, and the new border width compared with the previous one, and if they are different SD.XPOS and SD.YPOS are both zeroed. The border size is checked, and if valid the variables SD.XMIN to SD.YSIZE are updated to the new size. If the border is of width 0 or colour $80 then a return is made, otherwise the border is drawn with four rectangles of suitable size and position.

SD.WDEF — redefine a window: TRAP #3 with D0=$0D

Entry: D1.B   border colour
         D2.W   border width
         D3.W   timeout
         A0   channel ID
         A1   start of parameter block

Exit: D1   corrupted
         D2   preserved
         D3   preserved
         A0   preserved
         A1   corrupted
         A2   preserved

Errors: −1   not complete
          −4   out of range as window too large
          −6   invalid channel ID

Action: The specified window is redefined according to the supplied parameters — the A1 block format is:

0(A1)   window width
2(A1)   window depth
4(A1)   x position
6(A1)   y position

First the cursor is homed and each parameter checked to make sure the window is not greater than 512 × 256 in size. The border is then dealt with in a similar way to SD.BORDR above. Nothing is put on the screen unless a non-zero border size is specified.

SD.CURE — enable cursor: TRAP #3 with D0=$0E

Entry: D3.W   timeout
           A0.L   channel ID

Exit: D1   corrupted
           D2   preserved
           D3   preserved
           A0   preserved
           A1   corrupted
           A2   preserved

Errors: −1   not complete
           −4   out of range if cursor will not fit in window
           −6   invalid channel ID

Action: The cursor in the specified window is enabled. This is done automatically when a 'read line' or 'edit line' trap is called. The cursor may or may not flash, depending on whether or not it is the current input channel (defined by pressing CTRL C to cycle around every waiting channel).

If SD.CURF is positive, then the cursor is already enabled so a premature exit is made, else any pending newlines are activated, and a check is then made to ensure that there is room in the window for all of the cursor to be shown. SD.CURF is set to 1, then the cursor itself is printed in the window.

SD.CURS — suppress cursor: TRAP #3 with D0=$0F

Entry: D3.W   timeout
           A0.L   channel ID

Exit: D1   corrupted
           D2   preserved
           D3   preserved
           A0   preserved
           A1   corrupted
           A2   preserved

Errors: −1   not complete
           −4   out of range if existing cursor was too big for window
           −6   invalid channel ID

67

Action: The cursor in the specified window is disabled.

If the cursor is already suppressed then a premature exit is made, otherwise SD.CURF is zeroed and the cursor 'unprinted' from the screen.

SD.POS — position cursor at character location: TRAP #3 with D0=$10

Entry:	D1.W	x position
	D2.W	y position
	D3.W	timeout
	A0.L	channel ID

Exit:	D1	corrupted
	D2	preserved
	D3	preserved
	A0	preserved
	A1	corrupted
	A2	preserved

Errors:	−1	not complete
	−4	out of range as window not large enough
	−6	invalid channel ID

Action: The cursor is positioned within the window at the specified character position. Any pending newlines are cancelled.

Both parameters are multiplied by the current cursor size, then checked before being stored in SD.XPOS and SD.YPOS. If the screen is in mode 8 then SD.XPOS is made even. Finally SD.NLSTA is zeroed.

SD.TAB — set horizontal cursor position: TRAP #3 with D0=$11

Entry:	D1.W	x position in characters
	D3.W	timeout
	A0.L	channel ID

Exit:	D1	corrupted
	D2	preserved
	D3	preserved
	A0	preserved
	A1	corrupted
	A2	preserved

Errors:	−1	not complete
	−4	out of range as window too narrow
	−6	invalid channel ID

Action: The horizontal cursor position is set to the specified character position, and any pending newlines are cancelled.

The value of SD.YPOS is read into D2, then control continues into SD.POS.

SD.NL — move cursor to new character line: TRAP #3 with D0=$12

Entry:	D3.W	timeout
	A0.L	channel ID

Exit:	D1	corrupted
	D2	preserved
	D3	preserved
	A0	preserved
	A1	corrupted
	A2	preserved

Errors:	−1	not complete
	−4	out of range if at bottom of window
	−6	invalid channel ID

Action: The cursor is moved to the start of the next character line down the window. If the cursor is already at the bottom of the window, then 'out of range' occurs.

Move cursor by character square: TRAP #3
SD.PCOL — D0=$13: cursor left
SD.NCOL — D0=$14: cursor right
SD.PROW — D0=$15: cursor up
SD.NROW — D0=$16: cursor down

Entry:	D3.W	timeout
	A0.L	channel ID

Exit:	D1	corrupted
	D2	preserved
	D3	preserved
	A0	preserved

A1   corrupted

A2   preserved

Errors: −1   not complete

           −4   out of range if cursor would pass out of window

           −6   invalid channel ID

Action: The cursor is moved one character in any direction. An error occurs if the new cursor position would be outside the window.

SD.XPOS and SD.YPOS are altered by adding or subtracting SD.XINC or SD.YINC, and checked to ensure they are valid. The cursor is not moved if an error occurs. Any pending newlines are cancelled.

SD.PIXP — position cursor by pixel: TRAP #3 with D0=$17

Entry: D1.W   x position

           D2.W   y position

           D3.W   timeout

           A0.L   channel

Exit: D1   corrupted

          D2   preserved

          D3   preserved

          A0   preserved

          A1   corrupted

          A2   preserved

Errors: −1   not complete

           −4   out of range as position is not within window

           −6   invalid channel ID

Action: The cursor is positioned to the pixel position specified, so long as it lies inside the window. Any pending newlines are cancelled by this trap.

The values are checked to make sure they are in range, then put into SD.XPOS and SD.YPOS and SD.NLSTA is zeroed.

Scroll part or all of a window: TRAP #3

SD.SCROL — D0=$18: scroll whole window

SD.SCRTP — D0=$19: scroll top window

SD.SCRBT — D0=$1A: scroll bottom of window

Entry:	D1.W	number of pixels to scroll
	D3.W	timeout
	A0.L	channel ID

Exit:	D1	corrupted
	D2	preserved
	D3	preserved
	A0	preserved
	A1	corrupted
	A2	preserved

Errors:	−1	not complete
	−6	invalid channel ID

Action: A section of the screen is scrolled up (if D1<0) or down (if D0>0) the desired number of pixels. Pixel lines vacated by the scroll are set to the window's paper colour. The top of the screen is defined as the pixel line above the cursor up to the top of the window. The bottom of the screen lies from the line below the cursor to the bottom line of the window. No parameters in the channel definition block are altered.

Pan part or all of window: TRAP #3
SD.PAN — D0=$1B: pan all of window
SD.PANLN — D0=$1E: pan cursor line
SD.PANRT — D0=$1F: pan righthand of cursor line

Entry:	D1.W	distance to pan
	D3.W	timeout
	A0.L	channel ID

Exit:	D1	corrupted
	D2	preserved
	D3	preserved
	A0	preserved
	A1	corrupted
	A2	preserved

Errors:	−1	not complete
	−6	invalid channel ID

Action: A section of the window is panned vertically, with vacant pixels being set to the paper colour. The scroll will be to the left if D0<0, or to the right if D0>0. SD.PANLN will pan the whole of the cursor line of 10 or 20 pixels height by the whole width of the window. SD.PANRT will pan the righthand half of the cursor line.

Clear part or all of a window: TRAP #3
SD.CLEAR — D0=$20: clear all of window
SD.CLRTP — D0=$21: clear top of window
SD.CLRBT — D0=$22: clear bottom of window
SD.CLRLN — D0=$23: clear cursor line
SD.CLRRT — D0=$24: clear from cursor to end of cursor line

Entry:	D3.W	timeout
	A0.L	channel ID

Exit:	D1	corrupted
	D2	preserved
	D3	preserved
	A0	preserved
	A1	corrupted
	A2	preserved

Errors:	−1	not complete
	−6	invalid channel ID

Action: A section of the window is cleared to the window's paper colour. The sections of the screen follow the same definitions as for the scrolling and panning traps.

SD.FOUNT — redefine the character fonts: TRAP #3 with D0=$25

Entry:	D3.W	timeout
	A0.L	channel ID
	A1.L	font 1
	A2.L	font 2

Exit:	D1	corrupted
	D2	preserved
	D3	preserved
	A0	preserved
	A1	corrupted
	A2	preserved

Errors:	−1	not complete
	−6	invalid channel ID

Action: The fonts used for the window are set to the specified values, or to the respective default values for each font if either address register is zero. Each channel has two character fonts, each of which conforms to this layout:

byte 0   code of first character
byte 1   number of characters in font
bytes 2–$0A   first character pattern
bytes $0B–$13   second character pattern

and so on for each character. There are two fonts in the ROM — the first starts like:

DC.B $1F   first character
DC.B $60   number of characters
DC.B %01010100   first character — the graphic square
DC.B %00101000   defined in binary for clarity
DC.B %01010100
DC.B %00101000

and covers the ASCII characters from 31 (the square) to 127 (the copyright message). The second font starts like:

DC.B $7F   first character
DC.B $40   number of characters
DC.B %01010100   pattern for second character 127
DC.B %00101000

and covers the characters from 127 (the square) to 191, which are the foreign characters. When printing, the routine checks to see if the character is in the first font, and if it is then the routine uses that character. If not, the routine checks the second font, and uses that if the character is there, but if the routine can find the character in neither font, it uses the first character in the second font. Each character takes nine bytes, with each byte defining the printed pattern. Bits 6 to 2 inclusive are used for the character and, as the printing routine uses characters sized 10 × 6 pixels, it always puts a blank line at the top of a character. Character widths of 8, 12 and 16 pixels and the height of 20 pixels are achieved by manipulating each font, not by storing different fonts for different sizes as may be expected. With the standard fonts, character 127 prints as a copyright symbol from font 1, overriding the square in font 2. The second square is used for the invalid character codes.

QL colours

The QL has up to eight colours plus Flash available on screen, and each colour is denoted by a number thus:

73

	MODE 4	MODE 8
0	black	black
1	black	blue
2	red	red
3	red	magenta
4	green	green
5	green	cyan
6	yellow	white
7	white	yellow

To increase the range of colours, 'stipples' are available, which mix the colour in the lowest three bits together with bits 3 to 5, in a way defined by bits 6 and 7.

There are three different window colouring attributes that can be controlled on screen: there is the 'ink', which is the colour used for points plotted, lines and characters; the 'paper', which is used when clearing the screen, scrolling and panning; and the 'strip' which defines the background colour that characters are printed on.

SD.RECOL — recolour a window: TRAP #3 with D0=$26

Entry:	D3.W	timeout
	A0.L	channel ID
	A1.L	location of list of colours

Exit:	D1	corrupted
	D2	preserved
	D3	preserved
	A0	preserved
	A1	corrupted
	A2	preserved

Errors:	−1	not complete
	−6	invalid channel ID

Action: Each pixel colour is changed to another colour, specified by the colour list. The colour list consists of eight bytes, corresponding to the new colours for each of the old. Each byte should only range from 0 to 7 inclusive. If the screen is in mode 4, the contents of the odd locations are irrelevant. This is an attempt to simulate the hardware palette controls of other micros, but is very much slower.

Set colour attributes for window: TRAP #3
SD.SETPA — D0=$27: paper colour
SD.SETST — D0=$28: strip colour
SD.SETIN — D0=$29: ink colour

Entry:	D1.B	colour
	D3.W	timeout
	A0.L	channel ID

Exit:	D1	preserved
	D2	preserved
	D3	preserved
	A0	preserved
	A1	corrupted
	A2	preserved

Errors:	−1	not complete
	−6	invalid channel ID

Action: The appropriate parameter is stored in byte form in SD.PCOLR/ SCOLR/ICOLR and a suitable mask is calculated and stored in SD.PMASK/ SMASK/IMASK. Note that the PAPER trap is *not* the same as the Paper command in SuperBASIC — it does not set the strip colour as well, so if you want coloured backgrounds to your text then set the strip colour explicitly.

Set flash and underline for window: TRAP #3
SD.SETFL — D0=$2A: define flash mode
SD.SETUL — D0= $2B: define underline mode

Entry:	D1.B	0 turn off, <>0 turn on
	D3.W	timeout
	A0.L	channel ID

Exit:	D1	corrupted
	D2	preserved
	D3	preserved
	A0	preserved
	A1	corrupted
	A2	preserved

Errors:	−1	not complete
	−6	invalid channel ID

Action: The function is turned on or off by altering the bits in SD.CATTR appropriately.

SD.SETMD — define write mode: TRAP #3 with D0=$2C

Entry:	D1.W	mode
	D3.W	timeout
	A0.L	channel ID

Exit:	D1	corrupted
	D2	preserved
	D3	preserved
	A0	preserved
	A1	corrupted
	A2	preserved

Errors:	−1	not complete
	−6	invalid channel ID

Action: The value of D1 determines the writing mode thus:

−1   ink is EORed with the background
0   character background set to strip colour
1   character background set to transparent

Bits 2 and 3 of SD.CATTR are altered depending on the value of bits 0 and 1 of D1 respectively.

SD.SETSZ — define windows character size: TRAP #3 with D0=$2D

Entry:	D1.W	character width:
		0: 6 pixels
		1: 8 pixels
		2: 12 pixels
		3: 16 pixels
	D2.W	character height:
		0: 10 pixels
		1: 20 pixels
	D3.W	timeout
	A0.L	channel ID

Exit:	D1	corrupted
	D2	preserved

D3	preserved
A0	preserved
A1	corrupted
A2	preserved

Errors:	−1	not complete
	−6	invalid channel ID

Action: The character size is set to suit the parameters. In mode 8, attempts to set six or eight pixel spacing will be converted to 12 and 16 pixel spacing. The screen drivers can support variable width characters, but this trap allows only those given.

SD.XINC and SD.YINC are set to suit the values of D1–2, then they are checked to make sure the new size of cursor will fit within the window at the cursor's current position. If the cursor would fall off the righthand edge, a newline is done: if the cursor would fall off the top of the window, the window is scrolled down by 10 pixels and 10 is subtracted from SD.YPOS so the cursor position moves with it. Bit 0 of D2 is copied into bit 4 of SD.CATTR, and bits 0 and 1 of D1 copied into bits 5 and 6 of SD.CATTR.

SD.FILL — plot a solid block of colour: TRAP #3 with D0=$2E

Entry:	D1.B	colour of block
	D3.W	timeout
	A0.L	channel ID
	A1.L	location of parameter block

Exit:	D1	corrupted
	D2	preserved
	D3	preserved
	A0	preserved
	A1	corrupted
	A2	preserved

Errors:	−1	not complete
	−4	out of range if block would fall off window
	−6	invalid channel ID

Action: A block of colour is drawn in the window according to the parameter block of four words:

0(A1)	block width
2(A1)	block depth

4(A1)   x coordinate of top left of block
6(A1)   y coordinate of top left of block

The size of the block is tested to see if it will fit, and then the actual block fill routine is called. The state of bit 3 of SD.CATTR is taken into account, allowing EORing of blocks within windows. For drawing horizontal and vertical lines this is faster than using the line routine, as this does not need to use the floating point routines.

SN.DONL — do pending newline: TRAP #3 with D0=$2F

Entry:	D3.W	timeout
	A0.L	channel ID

Exit:	D1	corrupted
	D2	preserved
	D3	preserved
	A0	preserved
	A1	corrupted
	A2	preserved
	A3	preserved

Errors:	−1	not complete
	−6	invalid channel ID

Action: If a newline is pending in the window then it will be carried out. This is particularly useful if you want to enable the cursor at the bottom of the screen after printing something out.

First SD.NLSTA is examined to see if any newlines are pending: if not, a premature exit is made. Next the routine SD.NL is called to do the newline, and if the cursor has reached the bottom of the window then the whole window is scrolled up SD.YINC pixels and SD.XPOS is zeroed. Regardless of where the cursor is, SD.NLSTA is always zeroed before returning, to show that the newline is no longer pending.

Graphics routines

All the preceding I/O calls for the screen are based on the pixel coordinate system, with every coordinate stored in pixels relative to the top left of the window. All of the following traps use the graphics coordinate system. This is based on a theoretical window size of 65536 square, with its origin placed anywhere relative to the window. Coordinates are expressed as floating point numbers from −32768 to 32767, and are scaled so that shapes have the same proportions in any screen mode. The scaling factor is initialised to 100, which gives an equal x–y ratio. With graphics functions, any point that does not fall within the window will not be plotted, and no error will occur. In addition, if a shape such as a circle is plotted near to the edge of the window, the points that lie within the window will be plotted, while those that don't will not. It is also possible to fill any non re-entrant shape while it is being plotted, by the use of a remarkably simple but effective fill algorithm.

As all these routines require floating point numbers, this would seem a good time to explain their format. Size bytes are required, with the first two bytes holding the exponent (with the top four bits always being zero), and the following four bytes holding the mantissa. The exponent is signed and offset by $1F, so the value of the number is the mantissa multiplied by 2 ↑ (exponent−$81F). Conversion from register values to floating point is covered in Chapter 8.

Graphics functions: TRAP #3
SD.POINT — D0=$30: plot a point
SD.LINE — D0=$31: draw a line
SD.ARC — D0=$32: draw an arc
SD.ELIPS — D0=$33: draw a circle or ellipse
SD.SCALE — D0=$34: define scale and origin
SD.GCUR — D0=$36: define text cursor position

Entry:	D3.W	timeout
	A0.L	channel ID
	A1.L	maths stack pointer

Exit:	D1	corrupted
	D2	preserved
	D3	preserved
	A0	preserved
	A1	corrupted
	A2	preserved

Errors:	−1	not complete
	−6	invalid channel ID

Action: Each function requires certain parameters on an arithmetic stack, pointed to by A1. The maths stack is 'upside down', just like the system stack, and there should be 240 bytes free on it for the routines to use. (Unlike other floating point routines, this does not require A1 to be stored relative to A6.) The format for each parameter is:

SD.POINT	0(A1)	y coordinate
	6(A1)	x coordinate
SD.LINE	0(A1)	y coordinate of end of line
	6(A1)	x coordinate of end of line
	$0C(A1)	y coordinate of start of line
	$12(A1)	x coordinate of start of line
SD.ARC	0(A1)	angle of arc
	6(A1)	y coordinate of end of arc
	$0C(A1)	x coordinate of end of arc
	$12(A1)	y coordinate of start of arc
	$18(A1)	x coordinate of start of arc
SD.ELIPSE	0(A1)	angle of rotation
	6(A1)	radius
	$0C(A1)	eccentricity (1 for a circle)
	$12(A1)	y coordinate of centre
	$18(A1)	x coordinate of centre
SD.SCALE	0(A1)	x position of graphics origin
	6(A1)	y position of graphics origin
	$0C(A1)	scale factor
SD.GCUR	0(A1)	graphics x coordinate
	6(A1)	graphics y coordinate
	$0C(A1)	horizontal pixel offset of cursor
	$12(A1)	vertical pixel offset of cursor

These traps are used by the SuperBASIC commands POINT, LINE, ARC, ELLIPSE/CIRCLE, SCALE and CURSOR (with four parameters), though the parameters are stored in the opposite order to the SuperBASIC arguments.

SD.FLOOD — enable/disable fill mode: TRAP #3 with D0=$35

Entry:	D1.L	0: switch off
		1: switch on or restart
		odd: switch off user vector
		even: switch on user vector
	D3.W	timeout
	A0.L	channel ID

Exit:	D1	corrupted
	D2	preserved
	D3	preserved
	A0	preserved
	A1	corrupted

A2	preserved
A3	preserved

Errors: −1   not complete
        −3   out of memory as insufficient room for fill buffer
        −6   invalid channel ID

Action: Fill mode for the specified window is switched on or off. A buffer is used to store plotted points to be joined up, and fill mode should be switched off after each shape has been completed, to save memory.

If the trap is for switching the mode off then, after checking that the mode was indeed on, the common heap space used is reclaimed, and SD.FMOD zeroed. If it was for switching on, then any existing heap space is reclaimed, SD.FMOD set to 1, and 1040 bytes of heap space claimed, and the address stored in SD.FBUF. If the parameter is not 0 or 1, then this signifies that a user fill vector is to be switched on or off: if the parameter is odd then SD.FUSE is zeroed, if it is even D1 is stored in SD.FUSE. User fill vectors would appear to be a means of using your own fill algorithm, but further details are not known at this time.

Changing screen mode

There is a manager trap for changing the screen mode:

MT.DMODE — set or read screen mode: TRAP #1 with D0=$10

Entry:	D1.B	0 to set mode 4
		8 to set mode 8
		−1 to read mode
	D2.B	0 to set 'monitor'
		1 to set 'TV'
		−1 to read display type

Exit:	D1.B	mode: 0 or 8
	D2.B	display: 0 or 1
	D3	preserved
	A0	preserved
	A1	preserved
	A2	preserved
	A3	preserved
	A4	corrupted (NB)

Errors: none

81

Action: The screen status can be read or set with this trap. The TV/ monitor option can be used to see whether F1 or F2 was pressed after the switch on, and should not really be changed at any other time. This can be a little hazardous at times — if for example one job changes the screen mode some other job may get terribly confused by this action, so use the trap with caution. The trap also has the unfortunate effect of changing any windows that have not had their colour attributes explicitly stated into black ink, black paper and black strip — this makes it somewhat difficult to read!

There are two system variables associated with this trap: SV.TVMOD contains 0 for 'TV' and 1 for 'monitor', and SV.MCSTA holds a copy of the current value of the hardware register which controls the screen. If a read operation is requested, these two variables are returned after suitable masking of unwanted bits. Setting the display type simply copies the value into SV.TVMOD, while the most interesting course of action is taken when a mode change is requested. To start with, the mode is changed by writing to the hardware register, the entire display is cleared to black, and then every channel is checked to see if it is a CON or SCR type. Every time that the ROM finds a channel that is, it re-does the colour masks to suit the new mode, does a CLS, alters SD.XINC, SD.YINC and bit 6 of SD.CATTR if necessary, and repeats this until all the channels have been examined.

Note: In current ROMs there is a bug in the SuperBASIC MODE procedure that corrupts SV.TVMOD.

Utility window channel opening

To help setting up window channels, there are three useful utilities, which should only be called in user mode.

UT.WINDW — open a window channel given name: vector $C4

Entry: A0.L   pointer to name
          A1.L   pointer to parameter block

Exit: D1   corrupted
          D2   corrupted
          D3   corrupted
          A0   channel ID
          A1   corrupted
          A2   corrupted
          A3   corrupted

Errors:	−3	out of memory
	−4	out of range (as window is off screen)
	−6	channel not opened (as too many)
	−12	bad name

Action: A channel is opened using the name starting at (A0) in usual format (ie a word defining its length, followed by the ASCII of the name itself). In addition, there should be an additional parameter block defining the colours for the window thus:

0(A1)	border colour
1(A1)	border width
2(A1)	paper and strip colour
3(A1)	ink colour

First a channel is opened, using IO.OPEN (and will be owned by the calling job). After this, the parameter list is read and SD.BORDR, SD.SETPA, SD.SETST, and SD.SETIN called with suitable values, and finally SD.CLEAR is called to clear the new window with its new colours. This should not be called in supervisor mode as the routine uses infinite timeouts for its traps.

UT.CON/UT.SCR — open a SCR or CON channel: vectors $C6/$C8

Entry:	A1.L	pointer to parameter block

Exit:	D1	corrupted
	D2	corrupted
	D3	corrupted
	A0	channel ID
	A1	corrupted
	A2	corrupted
	A3	corrupted

Errors:	−3	out of memory
	−4	out of range (as window is off screen)
	−6	channel not opened (as too many)

Action: A channel is opened and set up according to a parameter block:

0(A1)	border colour
1(A1)	border width
2(A1)	paper and strip colour
3(A1)	ink colour

4(A1)	width (word)
6(A1)	height (word)
8(A1)	x origin (word)
$A(A1)	y origin (word)

This takes similar action to UT.WINDW, except that a default SCR/CON channel is first opened and then re-defined using SD.WDEF.

Device MDV — the microdrives

This is the most complicated of all the device drivers, being the only directory-based one on the standard QL. The actual handling of bytes is handled by 'gap interrupts', using slave blocks controlled indirectly by the driver. MDV channel definition blocks conform exactly to the format described in the previous chapter, with no additional information. The physical definition block does contain this additional information:

$24	MD.FAIL	byte	failure count — every revolution for each operation this increases until reaching 4 (write/verify operations) or 8 (read)
$25		3 bytes	currently unused
$28	MD.MAP	255*2 bytes even byte odd byte	microdrive map, in pairs for each sector: −1 bad, −2 unused, −3 deletion pending block number
$226	MD.LSECT	word	last sector allocated
$228	MD.PENDG	256 words	map of pending operations, a word for each sector
$428	MD.END		end of physical definition block

The actual layout of data on the cartridge is based on 512-byte sectors, of which there can be (theoretically) up to 255. Each sector has certain other parts to it, starting with the sector header. This has a $FF byte to begin with; then a byte for the sector number; followed by 10 bytes of the cartridge name; two bytes of a random number; and then finally two bytes of checksum. There is a short gap; followed by the block header, which is a file number byte; a block number byte; then two bytes of checksum. After another gap comes the sector itself, of 512 data bytes, and two bytes of checksum. Each section is preceded by a preamble, to synchronise the hardware. When a cartridge is firstly formatted, dummy data gets written to all sectors, then read back, so that a map of faulty sectors can be created, which itself is held in a special file.

Each file has a file number, from 0 to 240, but there are additionally two special file numbers — 248 for the directory file and 253 for an unused or bad block. Following the file number is a block number, ranging from 0 to 255, which stores which part of a file the block is: for example, block 0 holds bytes 0 to 511, block 1 holds 512 to 1023, and so on. (As each file is preceded by a 64-byte header in block number 0, this correspondence is not the same for actual data read or written to the file.)

Sector number 0 is special in that it holds the microdrive map, followed by a byte of the most recently allocated sector on the cartridge, and is copied into and out of MD.MAP to MD.LSECT.

There is one special file, which is the directory. This holds a copy of every file's header sequentially in file numeric order, and can be read just like any other file.

When used for QDOS I/O, there is one time when slave blocks are not usually used — when a 'Load bytes' trap is issued. In this case, sectors are read 'randomly' with interrupts disabled, in the same way that the Spectrum loads bytes. As a result, multi-tasking can get temporarily held up when this happens.

Microdrive physical I/O

Wherever possible, it is recommended that the QDOS I/O traps are used for accessing the microdrives. However, if necessary, there are a number of low level I/O routines, but they are very difficult to use for two reasons — first, the important motor control routine is not vectored, and second, there is the critical timing problem.

The next release of QDOS will have the motor routines vectored but, if using QDOS 1.02 or 1.03, the routines have to be called directly. To see where the routine is, it is recommended that MT.INF is used to find the ROM type, and then one of the locations called. Then, when QDOS 1.04 and subsequent versions appear, the relevant vectors can be called instead. For now, though, they have to be called directly.

It would be an understatement to say that the read routines are difficult to use. This is because the inter-sector gap has to be just at the position of the head at the time of the call, otherwise an error will occur. It can be useful to test bit 0 of $18021, which when set will help get in sync.

Note that all these routines require interrupts to be off (by OR.W #$0700,SR which is a privileged instruction), and A3 has to contain the microdrive control register. Beware of using these routines while QDOS is still doing a microdrive operation under interrupts — it is best to test SV.MDRUN at $280EE to wait for QDOS to finish its I/O, by which time its value will be zero.

MD.SELECT — switch a motor on: $2B64 (1.02)/$2B70 (1.03)

Entry: D1.W   motor number, 1–8
            A3.L $18020

Exit: D1   corrupted
          D2   corrupted
          D3   preserved
          A0   preserved
          A1   preserved
          A2   preserved
          A3   preserved

Errors: none (ignore D0 on return)

Action: The relevant microdrive motor is turned on, and all others turned off. This routine cannot be copied to RAM to create a ROM independent version, because the timing constants would have to be altered. Further, altering them will do no good as external RAM packs are unlikely to run at the same speed as the internal RAM!

MD.DESEL — switch all motors off: $2B5E (1.02)/$2B6A (1.03)

Entry: A3.L $18020

Exit: D1   corrupted
           D2   corrupted
           D3   preserved
           A0   preserved
           A1   preserved
           A2   preserved
           A3   preserved

Errors: none (ignore value of D0 on return)

Action: All the microdrive motors are turned off.

MD.SECTR — read a sector header: vector $12A

Entry: A1.L   start of buffer
           A3.L $18020

Exit: D1   corrupted
           D2   corrupted
           D3   corrupted
           D4   corrupted
           D6   corrupted

D7.B   sector number
A0   corrupted
A1   updated pointer (=old A1+15)
A2   corrupted
A3   preserved
A4   corrupted

Errors: ignore value of D0 — errors are handled by multiple return addresses

Action: This vector should be called with code like:

MOVE.W $12A,A0
JSR $4000(A0)
BRA.S BADMEDIUM
BRA.S BADHEADER
BRA.S OK

as this has three possible return addresses. On a correct return the buffer has 14 bytes filled:

$FF
sector number
10 bytes of filename
2 bytes of random number at time of format

A 'bad medium' return will occur if a preamble signal cannot be found on the tape, and 'bad header' will occur if the first byte is not $FF.

MD.READ — read a sector: vector $124

Entry: A1.L   start of buffer
            A3.L $18020

Exit: D1.L   file number
            D2.L   block number
            D3   corrupted
            D4   corrupted
            D6   corrupted
            D7.B   sector number
            A0   corrupted
            A1   updated pointer
            A2   corrupted
            A3   preserved
            A4   corrupted

Errors: ignore value of D0 — errors are handled by multiple return addresses

Action: This vector should be called with code like:

MOVE.W $124,A0
JSR $4000(A0)
BRA.S FAILED
BRA.S OK

as this has two possible return addresses. On a correct return the buffer has 512 bytes of data, read from the sector. A 'failed' error can be caused either by a lack of suitable preamble, or if the checksum fails.

MD.VERIN — verify a sector: vector $128

Entry:	A1.L	start of buffer
	A3.L	$18020

Exit:	D1.B	file number
	D2.B	block number
	D3	corrupted
	D4	corrupted
	D6	corrupted
	D7	corrupted
	A0	corrupted
	A1	updated pointer
	A2	corrupted
	A3	preserved
	A4	corrupted

Errors: ignore value of D0 — multiple returns used instead

Action: This should be called with code like:

MOVE.W $128,A0
JSR $4000 (A0)
BRA.S FAILED
BRA.S OK

The 'failed' error can be caused by a lack of preamble, a verification failure, or a checksum error. As this will attempt to verify the next sector to pass the head, you should use MD.SECTR first, to wait until the desired sector header has just passed the head, then this will attempt to read the data block following it.

MD.WRITE — write a sector: vector $126

Entry: A1.L   start of buffer
          A3.L $18020

Exit: D1   corrupted
        D2   corrupted
        D3   corrupted
        D4   corrupted
        D5   corrupted
        D6   corrupted
        A0   corrupted
        A1   updated pointer to buffer
        A2   corrupted
        A3   preserved
        A4   corrupted

Errors: none — ignore D0 on exit

Action: Before calling this, a word containing the file number (high byte) and the block number (low byte) should be pushed on the stack. (The extra word is not removed by the routine.) The data in the buffer, together with the word containing the file number and block number, are written on to the tape. The routine writes at the current position, so using this without MD.SECTR to position the tape will probably corrupt the tape.

This should be called with code like:

```
MOVE.W NOS, – (A7)    file and block number
MOVE.W $126, A0
JSR $4000 (A0)        call it
ADDQ.L #2, A7         remove extra
```

CHAPTER 6
Exceptions, Interrupts and the Job Scheduler

The 68008 has up to 256 exception handlers, for controlling various aspects of the machine, such as interrupts and hardware faults. Unfortunately the QL is prevented from using some of these because of the way the vector table starting at $00000 has been configured, though this may be improved in later versions of QDOS. Certain exceptions may be defined by the programmer. The exceptions that are implemented are:

Bus error: The additional words stacked are skipped over, and a return from exception made. A bus error should never occur on the QL as no hardware memory management is present.

Address error: Normally similar action is taken as with a bus error, which may or may not cause a system crash, depending on where within the instruction the odd word access occurred. This can be re-defined via RAM vector 0, in which case the format of the stacked data will be:

$C(A7) value of PC which caused the error
8(A7)   old value of status register (word)
6(A7)   instruction register — first word of offending instruction
4(A7)   address accessed in error
0(A7)   access type (word) — bits 0–2 are the previous state of the function code pins on the processor, bit 3 is set only if the error occurred during exception processing, and bit 4 will be set for a memory read, or reset for a write. If an address or bus error occurs within one of their exception handlers the processor will enter the halted state, and remain stopped until a signal is applied to the RESET pin.

Illegal instruction: If an illegal instruction (excluding those starting $Axxx and $Fxxx) is executed, the exception handler normally just does an RTE, which causes the machine to lock up, as it re-executes the illegal instruction forever. It can be re-defined with RAM vector 4.

Divide by zero, CHK, and TRAPV: All these exceptions are normally ignored by doing an RTE, but can be re-defined with RAM vectors 8, $0C and $10 respectively. The address on the stack corresponds to the instruction after the relevant DIV, CHK or TRAPV instruction.

Privilege violation: This exception normally causes the machine to lock up, as an RTE is done which re-executes the privileged instruction forever. It can be re-defined with RAM vector $14, and the address on the stack is the location of the instruction following the privileged one.

Trace exception: This exception is normally ignored by doing an RTE, so if the T bit is set then the only result is that the whole machine slows down. This can be re-defined with RAM vector $18, in which case the address on the stack is the next instruction to be executed.

Spurious interrupt: This should never occur on the QL except perhaps after a hardware failure. It is ignored by doing an RTE.

Interrupt exceptions: The 68000 interrupt levels 1, 3, 4 and 6 are ignored, and cannot be triggered on the 68008. Level 2 is the main system interrupt, explained in detail shortly, level 5 is ignored, and level 7 is usually ignored but may be re-defined with RAM vector $1C. Level 7 interrupts can normally only be triggered by additional hardware. However, an early debugging tool has been left in the hardware, so that pressing CTRL ALT 2, 5 or 7 triggers the equivalent interrupt. A level 7 interrupt will usually cause the machine to lock up as it destroys the communication process between the 68008 and the 8049 IPC.

Traps #0 to #4: These are QDOS calls, and not re-directable in current versions of QDOS.

Traps #5 to #15: These are usually ignored, but can be re-defined with RAM vectors $20 to $48.

The line 1010 and line 1111 exceptions are potentially the most useful that are not currently usable on the QL, though this may change on subsequent versions: for example, the line 1010 exception is used on the Apple Macintosh as pseudo instructions for the system calls controlling the graphics and toolbox routines.

RAM exception vectors

Certain exceptions may be re-defined, using a table in RAM of long words. In QDOS 1.03 and earlier, the format of this table is:

0	address error
4	illegal instruction
8	division by zero
$0C	CHK instruction
$10	TRAPV instruction
$14	privilege violation
$18	trace exception
$1C	interrupt level 7
$20	trap #5
$24	trap #6
$28	trap #7
$2C	trap #8
$30	trap #9
$34	trap #10
$38	trap #11
$3C	trap #12
$40	trap #13
$44	trap #14
$48	trap #15

In subsequent versions of QDOS this list may be extended. Each job can have its own RAM exception vector table, and when a job is created it is given the exception table of the *creating* job, which may not be the same as the owner job. There is a QDOS call to set up a RAM exception table:

MT.TRAPV — set up a job's RAM exception table: TRAP #1 with D0=7

Entry: D1.L   job ID (or −1 for 'current job')
            A1.L   location of table

Exit: D1.L   job ID
            D2   preserved
            D3   preserved
            A0   start of job header
            A1   corrupted
            A2   preserved
            A3   preserved

Errors: −2   invalid job ID

Action: The RAM exception vector table location is stored in the appropriate job header.

RAM exception vectors use two system variables: SV.TRAPV stores

93

the current table while, in each job header, JB.TRAPV stores each table. If a table is not set up, these contain 0, which tells the exception handler in the ROM to ignore suitable exceptions. When a table is set up, the (start address)−$54 is stored in both SV.TRAPV and JB.TRAPV. When a re-definable exception occurs, QDOS checks SV.TRAPV and ignores the exception if zero. If SV.TRAPV is not zero, then it is used to calculate which long word is to be used as the exception routine, and a jump made to this.

As QL machine code has to be position independent, exception tables cannot contain absolute addresses, but have to be configured before the MT.TRAPV call using instructions something like:

```
LEA HANDLER(PC),A0
MOVE.L A0,xx(A1)
```

Writing exception handlers
When writing exception handlers there are a few things to be aware of, compared with writing the more usual code. The main difference is that the handler is always executed in supervisor mode, giving access to the usually privileged instructions. You are also free to change interrupt modes, as the final RTE restores the old value of the SR, including the interrupt mask. It's easy to do, but two of the best ways of crashing the QL are by writing an exception handler that either returns by RTS instead of RTE, or by not preserving enough registers. With the exception of the traps, all exception handlers should preserve all the register values, to prevent nasty problems cropping up.

When running in supervisor mode, be careful when calling QDOS. Some of the routines are not atomic, because they re-enter the scheduler, and if you do call such a routine in supervisor mode the system will crash. The other things to be very wary of are the timeouts used in the I/O traps. When in supervisor mode, *all I/O timeouts must be 0*, otherwise the IOSS will enter the scheduler if an operation returns 'not complete'.

Interrupt level 2
This is the main system interrupt, and is responsible for a multitude of things, including:

scanning the keyboard
reading and writing the RS232 ports
reading and writing microdrive cartridges
external interrupt
flashing the cursor
controlling the jobs via the scheduler

The interrupt normally occurs every 50th or 60th of a second, depending on the 'nationality' of the QL. The actions taken depend to a large extent on signals given by the 8049 IPC or one of the custom chips within the machine, and each action will now be covered in turn, to give a fuller understanding of this important aspect of QDOS.

The first thing that the interrupt handler does is to examine PC.INTR which is a byte read from one of the ULAs. Bit 0–4 will be set if certain hardware features are active, and each bit triggers its own handler. These handlers are:

Bit 0 — gap interrupt

This is responsible for reading and writing to the microdrives, using the slave blocks in RAM. It is triggered by the electronics in the ULA detecting a gap of a tape passing a microdrive head. If during a sector read or write operation an error occurs, then a counter is incremented, and if it reaches 8 (for a read) or 4 (for a write or verify) then an attempt is made to print an error message of the cartridge name followed by 'bad or changed medium' on channel 0 or 1, then all slave blocks which refer to the suspect drive are marked as 'free to use'.

Bit 1 — interface interrupt

This is responsible for general input from the QL peripheral chips, and starts by reading the input status of the IPC, using command #1. Both SV.WP and SV.SOUND are updated to show the current write-protect and sound status, then the keyboard scanned if a key is being held down. Both RS232 ports are then examined and read, provided that there exists a suitable queue for each, and that there is valid data waiting to be read.

Reading the keyboard is done via the IPC, with the 68008 looking after its conversion to ASCII, and the key repeating rates. So long as the key pressed is not a 'special' one, it is put into the current keyboard queue. The 'special' keys are Break, CTRL F5, Caps Lock, ALT, and CTRL C.

When Break is pressed, SV.SCRST is zeroed, to make sure the screen is 'active', and then BV.BRK is set to show SuperBASIC that Break has been pressed. If it was waiting for an I/O operation to complete, then SuperBASIC's JB.STAT is zeroed, to release the job. This is so that SuperBASIC can have incomplete I/O operations interrupted with Break. When CTRL F5 is pressed, SC.SCRST is inverted, as it is the toggle control for disabling window output. When Caps Lock is pressed, the SV.CAPS is inverted, and if SV.CSUB is non-zero then it is called as a subroutine. On pressing ALT, the character $FF is put in the queue directly followed by the key being held down at the same time as ALT. CTRL C is the default 'change keyboard queue' character, though it can be re-defined by altering SV.CQCH. When pressed, the cursor in the current window is enabled and the next queue in the list found, then SV.KEYQ updated to suit. Note that pressing CTRL F5, CTRL C, ALT on its own, or Caps Lock will *not* put anything into the keyboard queue.

Bit 2 — transmit interrupt

This controls transmission from both serial ports, provided that both bit 4 of SV.TMOD and bit 1 of PC.MCTRL are zero, preventing transmission if either microdrive buffer is not empty. If it is OK to transmit, then the appropriate queue address is found, using SV.SER1C or SV.SER2C, depending on bit 3 of SV.TMOD. Provided there is a queue, the channel definition block of the serial port is found, and SER.TXHS examined. If it shows that handshaking is to be used on output, then either the DTR (port 1) or CTS (port 2) is tested to see if the serial device is ready for input, and if it is then a byte is read from the queue and sent to the port. At the end of the routine, bit 3 of SV.TMOD is toggled, so that the other serial port is used on the next call, and the complete value of SV.TMOD is written out to the PC.TCTRL transmit register in the ULA.

Bit 3 — frame interrupt

This interrupt handles one or two of the QDOS linked lists, and also the very important job scheduler. SV.POLLM is incremented, then the entire 'polled list' executed, and an exit made if in supervisor mode. If not, the scheduler is entered, to re-schedule all the jobs if necessary. This is probably the most important piece of code in QDOS, and is covered in a moment. First we'll look at the polled list, what it does, and how to add to it.

The polled list

This is also known as the 50/60 Hz list, but the latter is a misnomer as it does not always occur as regularly as this would indicate. The polled list is a linked list whose main purpose is for handling interrupts from devices that cannot electronically signal their own interrupts. This is done by 'polling', so that the service routine checks its own peripheral by reading something from a status register, say, and taking special action if required. That said, there is nothing at all stopping you from using this for any other purpose. On power up, one item is put in this list, and there are system traps for linking and removing your own entries. The single list entry takes identical steps to the interface interrupt, namely reading the keyboard and RS232 ports. This is to make sure that these devices are scanned regularly.

MT.LPOLL — link a routine into the polled list: TRAP #1 with D0=$1C

Entry: A0.L   address of link

Exit: D1   preserved
           D2   preserved
           D3   preserved
           A0   preserved
           A1   corrupted
           A2   preserved
           A3   preserved

Errors: none

Action: A0 should point to two long words in RAM: the first long word will be used by QDOS to point to the next link, while the second should contain the address of the routine. The latter address *must* be set up before using this trap, in case a polled interrupt occurs before the job has a chance to set the address. As code has to be position independent, it requires lines like:

```
LEA ROUTINE(PC),A0
MOVE.L A0,4(A1)          store the address
MOVEQ #$1C,D0
TRAP #1                  do the trap
```

The link should be either in RESPR or the common heap. If in RESPR, the system is liable to crash should the area be collapsed, and if in the common heap the space *must* be owned by job 0, otherwise it will be reclaimed should the job be removed from the system. User entries in the list are called before the inbuilt polled service routine. Service routines are executed in supervisor mode, but an exit should always be made with RTS and never RTE. Calling this routine twice with the same link address will crash the machine, as it will never exit from the polled list.

There is also a complementary trap to remove entries from the list:

MT.RPOLL — remove entry from polled list: TRAP #1 with D0=$1D

Entry: A0.L   address of link

Exit: D1   preserved
           D2   preserved
           D3   preserved
           A0   preserved

A1   corrupted

A2   preserved

A3   preserved

Errors: none

Action: The specified link is removed from the polled list. Note that no checks are made on the validity of the link, so if the address pointed to by A0 is not really a link in the list then the system is liable to crash.

When a polled routine is called, the processor is in supervisor state, and within the routine most registers can be used. However, the value of A6 is always $28000 and *must not be altered*. On entry to the routine D3 contains 1, D0 contains −8, and A3 contains the assumed start of the device driver linkage block (ie address of link −8).

    When the whole polled list has been executed, a return is made if the processor was in supervisor mode at the time of the interrupt, otherwise the vitally important scheduler is entered.

The scheduler

This is probably the most important part of the QL ROM, as it controls execution and scheduling of all the jobs in the machine. It is entered either directly from the frame interrupt, or indirectly after certain non-atomic traps.

    To start with, all the current job's details are saved in its job header, including all the register values, and JB.PRIOR is tested to make sure that its only non-zero value is 1. The system random number SV.RAND is incremented, and then the scheduler linked list done (we will cover this later). The routine then finds the next job to have a share of the machine, by comparing various details in each job header as follows. JB.PRINC is examined and, as long as it's not zero (ie the job is active), JB.STAT is tested to see if it is zero. If it is zero, this is to be the next job to be re-started, else as long as the job is not suspended, then JB.STAT is decremented. If the new value of JB.STAT is zero or less then it is zeroed, and location JB.HOLD is zeroed as the job is about to be released. When a potentially new job has been found using the above method, JB.PRIOR is examined — if it is zero, then it is made 1, otherwise JB.PRINC gets added to it, to give a new priority. This value is the deciding factor when comparing jobs to see which one is to have control, and the new job header location is stored in SV.JBPNP, and is re-started by 'unloading' the stored register values in the header.

The scheduler list

This is a linked list of tasks to be executed every time the scheduler itself is entered. The list is roughly the same as the polled list except it does not get called if the machine is in supervisor mode. On power-up, there are three entries in this list — one task to flash the cursor, one to handle transmit interrupts, and the last the very important 'do waiting I/O' routine.

The 'flash the cursor' routine starts by examining SV.KEYQ for the current keyboard queue, making a quick exit if for some reason there is no queue. If there is, then the cursor status in SV.FSTAT is examined: if it is zero then it is reset to 12 and a return made. If it is non-zero, then it is decremented: if it is then zero the cursor is 'flashed', and then SV.FSTAT set to 12. The flash rate is thus fixed at 12/50ths (or 12/60ths) of a second.

The transmit interrupt routine is the same as that described previously, controlling transmission from the serial ports.

The third item in the list is the 'waiting I/O' routine. Its purpose is to handle non-zero and infinite timeouts for trap #3 operations until they either timeout or complete. It uses SV.CHPNT to cycle round all the channels, examining each CH.STAT until it finds a non-zero one. On finding a channel that is waiting on I/O, CH.JOBWT is read for the ID, the suitable entry in the job table found, and if the job has been removed then CH.STAT is zeroed and a return made. Assuming the job is still in the system, then CH.ACTN is read, along with the jobs register values, then the relevant I/O routine called in the device driver pointed to by CH.DRIVR. On return, the register values are stored back in the job header along with the error value from D0, and if it still returns 'not complete' then a return is made, otherwise the I/O operation is deemed to be finished and CH.STAT and JB.STAT are both zeroed before returning.

There are two traps for linking and unlinking your own tasks into the scheduler list:

MT.LSCHD — link task into scheduler list: TRAP #1 with D0=$1E

Entry: A0.L   address of link

Exit: D1   preserved
            D2   preserved
            D3   preserved
            A0   preserved
            A1   corrupted
            A2   preserved
            A3   preserved

Errors: none

Action: The double long word link at location (A0) is added to the scheduler linked list. The rules described previously for polled task links apply to scheduler links too.

There is a complementary trap to remove a link:

MT.RSCHD — remove entry from scheduler list: TRAP #1 with D0=$1F

Entry: A0.L   location of link

Exit: D1   preserved
          D2   preserved
          D3   preserved
          A0   preserved
          A1   corrupted
          A2   preserved
          A3   preserved

Errors: none

Action: The link is removed from the scheduler linked list.

When a scheduler task is called, the processor is in supervisor state, and D0.L will be −16, D3.B will be the old value of SV.POLLM, and A6 will be $28000 (and should not be altered). A3 is the assumed start of the device driver linkage block (ie address of link −16).

External interrupts
These can only be triggered by additional hardware, and have a linked list of tasks that is empty after a switch-on. There are two associated system traps:

MT.LXINT — link a routine into external interrupt list: TRAP #1 with D0=$1A

Entry: A0.L   location of link

Exit: D1   preserved
          D2   preserved

D3	preserved
A0	preserved
A1	corrupted
A2	preserved
A3	preserved

Errors: none

Action: The double long word link is added to the external interrupt task list. The usual rules apply for the link as described under the section Polled list.

MT.RXINT — remove item from external interrupt list: TRAP #1 with D0=$1B

Entry: A0.L   location of link

Exit:
D1	preserved
D2	preserved
D3	preserved
A0	preserved
A1	corrupted
A2	preserved
A3	preserved

Errors: none

Action: The link is removed from the external interrupt linked list.

When an external interrupt routine is called, the processor is in supervisor state, with D0.L=0 and A6=$28000. All registers can be used, with the usual exception of A6.

101

CHAPTER 7
QDOS Utilities

There are various QDOS system calls that don't slot into any of the previous chapters, and these will now be covered under this general title. They are concerned with such things as the real-time clock, message printing, base conversion, and memory usage.

The real-time clock
One of the ULAs in the QL has a clock which stores the time in seconds, with a base date of January 1, 1961, 00:00:00. As this is a long word, it will work well into the 21st century, which should cover most needs. The original QL specification mentioned the inclusion of a battery to keep the clock going when the power to the QL was removed, but unfortunately this was not included on the final production machines. Thus every time you want to use the clock it has to be set after a switch-on. There are various traps to read and write to the clock, and for converting the result into a more meaningful form.

MT.SCLCK — set the time: TRAP #1 with D0=$14

Entry: D1.L   time (in seconds)

Exit: D1   preserved
             D2   corrupted
             D3   corrupted
             A0   corrupted
             A1   preserved
             A2   preserved
             A3   preserved

Errors: none

Action: The clock is set to the specified time. Do not attempt simply to write the long word into the clock's register location, as this will simply zero it.

Firstly the time is zeroed, then a rotating byte put into the register 256 times for each second.

MT.RCLCK — read time from clock: TRAP #1 with D0=$13

Entry:	none	

Exit:	D1.L	time (in seconds)
	D2.L	corrupted (actually=D1)
	D3	preserved
	A0	corrupted
	A1	preserved
	A2	preserved
	A3	preserved

Errors:	none

Action: The time is read into D1. The clock register is scanned and when two consecutive readings are the same a return is made. This is to prevent possible mis-readings as the clock has an internal carry.

MT.ACLCK — adjust the time: TRAP #1 with D0=$15

Entry:	D1.L	adjustment required (in seconds)

Exit:	D1	new time (in seconds)
	D2	corrupted
	D3	corrupted
	A0	corrupted
	A1	preserved
	A2	preserved
	A3	preserved

Errors:	none

Action: The adjustment is made to the value of the clock. If the adjustment is negative then the clock's value will be decremented appropriately.

First the time is read, as in MT.RCLCK, the displacement is added, and then the clock is set, as in MT.SCLCK. Up to QDOS 1.03, no special action is taken if the adjustment is 0, contrary to other documentation.

CN.DATE — convert time into ASCII: vector $EC

Entry:	D1.L	time (in seconds)
	A1.L	pointer to maths stack (relative to A6)

Exit:	D1	preserved
	D2	preserved
	D3	preserved
	A0	preserved
	A1	new stack (=old A1–$16)
	A2	preserved
	A3	preserved

Errors: none

Action: The time is converted into an ASCII string of 20 characters in the form 'year mon dt hr:mn:sc'. The operation of the maths stack is covered in the next chapter but, briefly, everything is relative to A6: after the string operation the word at location (A1,A6) is the length, then starting at 2(A1,A6) are the ASCII bytes of the string. After this routine the string is 20 bytes in length, and the system call requires 22 bytes of space on the stack (which follows usual 68008 protocols in being 'upside down').

CN.DAY — convert time to day of week: vector $EE

Entry:	D1.L	time (in seconds)
	A1.L	maths stack (relative to A6)

Exit:	D1	preserved
	D2	preserved
	D3	preserved
	A0	preserved
	A1	new stack (=old A1–6)
	A2	preserved
	A3	preserved

Errors: none

Action: The value of the time is used to calculate which day of the week it is, and the result returned as a three-character string on the maths stack (ie (A1,A6) contains 3, then 2(A1,A6) onwards hold the three bytes). This requires six free bytes on the maths stack.

105

Unfortunately there are no QDOS routines to convert the other way, from date in usual format into the time in seconds, though the method can be borrowed from the way SuperBASIC does this for its SDATE command, thus:

Program 7.1: The SDATE Calculations

```
*  assumes the maths stack (A1) contains 6 words
*  being year, month, day, hours, minutes, seconds
*  (this listing generated with disassembler from
*  ROM version JM - 1.03)

* ROM contents (c) Sinclair Research 1983

0620A 20369800          MOVE.L  $00(A6,A1.L),D0   year
0620E 04800000          SUBI.L  #1961,D0          relative to 1961
06212 07A9
06214 2200              MOVE.L  D0,D1
06216 C2FC016D          MULU    #365,D1           work out days
0621A 24369804          MOVE.L  $04(A6,A1.L),D2   month
0621E 80FC0004          DIVU    #$0004,D0         test for leap year
06222 4840              SWAP    D0
06224 0C400003          CMPI.W  #$0003,D0
06228 6608              BNE.S   L06232
0622A 0C420002          CMPI.W  #$0002,D2
0622E 6F02              BLE.S   L06232
06230 5281              ADDQ.L  #1,D1             add in extra day
06232 4240    L06232    CLR.W   D0
06234 4840              SWAP    D0
06236 D280              ADD.L   D0,D1             total so far
06238 5382              SUBQ.L  #1,D2             dec month number
0623A E342              ASL.W   #1,D2             double it
0623C 45FB202E          LEA     L0626C(PC,D2.W),A2 get month length index
06240 4280              CLR.L   D0
06242 3012              MOVE.W  (A2),D0           get month cumulative total
06244 D280              ADD.L   D0,D1             add to total
06246 D2B69808          ADD.L   $08(A6,A1.L),D1   add in the day in the month
0624A 5341              SUBQ.W  #1,D1             decrement
0624C 7018              MOVEQ   #24,D0
0624E 6134              BSR.S   L06284            convert days to hours
06250 D2B6980C          ADD.L   $0C(A6,A1.L),D1   add hours
06254 703C              MOVEQ   #60,D0
06256 612C              BSR.S   L06284            convert to minutes
06258 D2B69810          ADD.L   $10(A6,A1.L),D1   add minutes
0625C 6126              BSR.S   L06284            convert to seconds
0625E D2B69814          ADD.L   $14(A6,A1.L),D1   add seconds
06262 7014              MOVEQ   #$14,D0
06264 4E41              TRAP    #$01              set the time
06266 7000              MOVEQ   #$00,D0           no error
06268 4A80    L06268    TST.L   D0
0626A 4E75              RTS                       quit

* this is a table giving the cumulative totals of the lengths
* of every month
0626C 0000001F L0626C   DC.W    $0000,$001F       Jan,Feb
06270 003B005A          DC.W    $003B,$005A       Mar,Apr
06274 00780097          DC.W    $0078,$0097       May,Jun
06278 00B500D4          DC.W    $00B5,$00D4       Jul,Aug
0627C 00F30111          DC.W    $00F3,$0111       Sep,Oct
06280 0130014E          DC.W    $0130,$014E       Nov,Dec

* routine to do 16 bit multiply D1=D1*D0
06284 6122    L06284    BSR.S   L062A8
06286 2604              MOVE.L  D4,D3
06288 4840              SWAP    D0
0628A 4841              SWAP    D1
```

```
0628C  611A          BSR.S   L062A8
0628E  2404          MOVE.L  D4,D2
06290  4840          SWAP    D0
06292  4843          SWAP    D3
06294  6112          BSR.S   L062A8
06296  6116          BSR.S   L062AE
06298  4840          SWAP    D0
0629A  4841          SWAP    D1
0629C  610A          BSR.S   L062A8
0629E  610E          BSR.S   L062AE
062A0  4843          SWAP    D3
062A2  4840          SWAP    D0
062A4  2203          MOVE.L  D3,D1
062A6  4E75          RTS

*  does  D4=D1*D0  (word)
062A8  2800  L062A8  MOVE.L  D0,D4
062AA  C8C1          MULU    D1,D4
062AC  4E75          RTS

*  does  D3=D3+D4  (word)
*        D2=D2+(D4 AND $FFFF0000)+X
062AE  D644  L062AE  ADD.W   D4,D3
062B0  4244          CLR.W   D4
062B2  4844          SWAP    D4
062B4  D584          ADDX.L  D4,D2
062B6  4E75          RTS
```

Message printing routines

UT.MTEXT — print message on channel: vector $D0

Entry:	A0.L	channel ID
	A1.L	start of message

Exit:	D1	corrupted
	D2	corrupted
	D3	corrupted
	A0	preserved
	A1	corrupted
	A2	preserved
	A3	preserved

Errors: any errors from I/O operations

Action: The specified message is sent to the channel, and must be in the form of a word — the length of the message, followed by the actual ASCII of the message. If A0 is non-zero, then the timeout is set to −1 (for 'wait until completion'), but to allow code running in supervisor mode there exists a special feature if A0=0. In this case, the timeout is 0: the routine is called, and if the I/O trap returns 'not complete' (ie the channel is already in use) then the same is attempted with channel $00010001. If this fails, too, then no message is actually printed, and a 'not complete' error return made. In addition, if A0=0 then SV.SCRST is zeroed to ensure the screen is active. Note that because of the timeouts *this must not be used in supervisor mode unless A0=0* as it will not be atomic.

Apart from dealing with the special case of A0=0, the code for this vector is basically

MOVE.W (A1)+,D2   get length
MOVEQ #7,D0   signal 'print string'
TRAP #3

UT.ERR — print error message on channel: vector $CC

Entry: D0.L   error code
          A0.L   channel ID

Exit: D0   preserved
          D1   preserved
          D2   preserved
          D3   preserved
          A0   preserved
          A1   preserved
          A2   preserved
          A3   preserved

Errors: any of the I/O errors

Action: The error message corresponding to the value in D0 is printed on the specified channel. As this uses UT.MTEXT *this must not be called in supervisor mode* unless A0=0.

If D0 is positive, no action is taken; otherwise the appropriate message is used from either the QDOS ROM or from an external device, and then printed using UT.MTEXT.

UT.ERR0 — print error message on channel 0: vector $CA

Entry: D0.L   error code

Exit: D0   preserved
          D1   preserved
          D2   preserved
          D3   preserved
          A0   preserved
          A1   preserved

A2   preserved
A3   preserved

Errors: any of the usual I/O errors

Action: The error message is printed on to channel 0, with a timeout of 0: if unsuccessful, an attempt is made to print it to channel $00010001. The routine uses UT.MTEXT as you may have expected. It's perfectly safe to call this one in supervisor mode. You may wonder what you can do if you want to print an error message in supervisor mode on another channel. Well, although there is no vector to do this, it is possible by reading certain parts from the above routine, as the problem is knowing where in the ROM the error messages are. The way to do it is as follows:

```
         TST.L D0
         BGE.S NOERR            if no error
         MOVE.L D0,A1
         ADD.L D0,D0
         BVS.S PRTSTR           if user-defined error message
         NEG.W D0               make it positive
         MOVE.W $CC,A0          usual routine start
         LEA $22(A0),A1         start of index to message
         MOVE.W –2(A1,D0.W),D0  read from index
         LEA 0(A1,D0.W),A1      start of error message
PRTSTR   MOVE.W (A1)+,D2        length
         MOVEQ #7,D0            print string
         MOVEQ #0,D3            timeout
         MOVE.L #CHANID,A0      channel ID
         TRAP #3               print it
NOERR    RTS
```

UT.MINT — print decimal number on channel: vector $CE

Entry: D1.W   value to print
           A0.L   channel ID

Exit: D1   corrupted
         D2   corrupted
         D3   corrupted
         A0   preserved
         A1   corrupted
         A2   corrupted
         A3   corrupted

Errors: all the possible I/O errors

Action: The word value of D1 is converted to a signed decimal number in ASCII, and printed on the specified channel. As this uses UT.MTEXT *it must not be called in supervisor mode unless A0=0.*

This uses another QDOS routine to convert the number into ASCII in a buffer on the stack, then prints it. *Note:* in current QDOS versions there is a remote possibility of the QL crashing if this is called from job 0 (SuperBASIC) as register A6 is zeroed for the duration of this routine; also, if it is called in user mode and another job gets created concurrently, then SuperBASIC will crash, usually taking the rest of the machine with it. A space is *not* printed after the number, contrary to other documentation.

Base conversions

There are many QDOS vectors to convert between various bases, but unfortunately several do not work in current versions of QDOS.

Convert into ASCII: vectors:
CN.FTOD — $F0: floating point
CN.ITOD — $F2: signed integer (word)

Entry:	A0.L	pointer to buffer for result (relative A6)
	A1.L	pointer to stack for value (relative A6)

Exit:	D1.L	length of result
	D2	preserved
	D3	preserved
	A0	location of last character in buffer+1 (relative A6)
	A1	location of updated stack (old A1–6 or A1–2)
	A2	preserved
	A3	preserved

Errors: none — ignore value of D0 on return

Action: The value on the maths stack is converted into ASCII in a buffer, into either a signed integer or floating point form.

Convert into ASCII: vectors:
CN.ITOBB — $F4: binary (8 bits)
CN.ITOBW — $F6: binary (16 bits)

CN.ITOBL — $F8: binary (32 bits)
CN.ITOHB — $FA: hex (8 bits)
CN.ITOHW — $FC: hex (16 bits)
CN.ITOHL — $FE: hex (32 bits)

Entry: A0.L   pointer to buffer for result (relative to A6)
          A1.L   pointer to maths stack for value
                 (relative to A6)

Exit: D1   preserved
          D2   preserved
          D3   preserved
          A0   pointer to end of buffer+1
          A1   pointer to new stack (old A1−1 or −2 or −4)
          A2   preserved

Errors: none — ignore value of D0 on exit

Action: The byte(s) on the maths stack are converted to a suitably-sized
ASCII sequence in a buffer.

Convert from ASCII: vectors:
CN.DTOF — $100: floating point
CN.DTOI — $102: signed word integer

Entry: D7.L   pointer to 1 past end of buffer (relative to A6)
          A0.L   pointer to buffer of characters (relative to A6)
          A1.L   pointer to maths stack for result (relative to A6)

Exit: D1   corrupted
          D2   corrupted
          D3   preserved
          D7   preserved
          A0   pointer to 1 past end of buffer =D7 on entry
                 (unless error)
          A1   pointer to new stack =old A1–2 or A1–6
                 (unless error)
          A2   corrupted
          A3   corrupted

Errors: −17   error in expression

Action: These convert a number in ASCII into a value on the maths stack.

111

If an error occurs then A0 and A1 return with their old values; otherwise they are updated.

Convert from ASCII: vectors:
CN.BTOIB — $104: binary (8 bits)
CN.BTOIW — $106: binary (16 bits)
CN.BTOIL — $108: binary (32 bits)
CN.HTOIB — $10A: hex (8 bits)
CN.HTOIW — $10C: hex (16 bits)
CN.HTOIL — $10E: hex (32 bits)

Entry:	D7.L	pointer to end of buffer (relative to A6) or 0
	A0.L	pointer to buffer of characters (relative to A6)
	A1.L	pointer to maths stack for result (relative to A6)

Exit:	D1	corrupted
	D2	corrupted
	D3	preserved
	D7	preserved
	A0	pointer to end of buffer (unless error)
	A1	pointer to new stack (unless error)
	A2	corrupted
	A3	corrupted

| *Errors:* | −17 | error in expression |

Action: These routines should convert values from an ASCII buffer into a value on the maths stack. Unfortunately, in current versions of QDOS they contain a large number of mistakes, and so do not work.

Memory usage
There are several system calls for memory allocation and control:

MM.ALCHP — allocate common heap: vector $C0

| *Entry:* | D1.L | number of bytes required |
| | A6 | system variables (=$28000) |

Exit:	D1.L	number of bytes allocated
	D2	corrupted
	D3	corrupted

A0.L	start of area allocated
A1	corrupted
A2	corrupted
A3	corrupted
A6	preserved

Errors: −3   out of memory

Action: This is an atomic version of MT.ALCHP, and *must only be called in supervisor mode*. This differs in that the header for the area allocated is not taken into account, and it is the responsibility of the calling code to set it. The main use for this trap is in device drivers, for allocating space for channel definition blocks for the Open operation. The area allocated is set to zero.

MM.RECHP — release common heap: vector $C2

Entry: A0.L   start of area to release
           A6.L   start of system variables (=$28000)

Exit: D1   corrupted
           D2   corrupted
           D3   corrupted
           A0   corrupted
           A1   corrupted
           A2   corrupted
           A3   corrupted
           A6   preserved

Errors: none

Action: This is an atomic version of MT.RECHP, and *must only be called in supervisor mode*. Again this does not take into account the usual headers of the common heap area.

UT.LINK — link into a list: vector $D2

Entry: A0.L   location of link
           A1.L   location of pointer to list

Exit: D1   preserved
           D2   preserved

D3	preserved
A0	preserved
A1	preserved
A2	preserved
A3	preserved

Errors: none

Action: Every list must have a pointer to its first element, equivalent to a system variable, whose address is passed in A1. At (A0) there should be two long words — the first is used by the routine to link to the next item, while the second is user-defined: in the case of the system linked lists, the long word is the address of the routine to call.

The link is added to the beginning of a list, and when a list is set up its pointer must be zero. The actual code to do this is so trivial that it's actually more efficient to do the same two instructions directly, namely:

MOVE.L (A1),(A0)   update the link
MOVE.L A0,(A1)   and update the pointer

UT.UNLNK — remove an item from linked list: vector $D4

Entry:	A0.L	location of link
	A1.L	location of pointer to list

Exit:	D1	preserved
	D2	preserved
	D3	preserved
	A0	preserved
	A1	corrupted
	A2	preserved
	A3	preserved

Errors: none

Action: The item is removed from the list by altering the link elements in the list.

UT.CSTR — compare two character strings: vector $E6

Entry:	D0.B	type of comparison
	A0.L	start of string 0 (relative to A6)
	A1.L	start of string 1 (relative to A6)

Exit:	D0.L	result: −1, 0 or 1
	D1	preserved
	D2	preserved
	D3	preserved
	A0	preserved
	A1	preserved
	A2	preserved
	A3	preserved

Errors: none — value returned in D0 is not an error code

Action: The two strings are compared with one another, the result returning in D0 — 0 if they are the same, −1 if string0<string1, or 1 if string0>string1. Each string must start on a word boundary, beginning with a word defining its length, followed by its characters. There are four types of comparisons:

type 0   characters are compared directly
type 1   the case of the characters is ignored
type 2   taking numeric values into account
type 3   a combination of types 1 and 2

When characters are compared, their 'value' is not their ASCII code, but is based on this order:

space ! "# $ % & ' ( ) * + , − / : ; <=> ? @ [\ ] ↑ _ £ { | } ~ ©.
0 1 2 3 4 5 6 7 8 9
A a B b C c D d E e F f G g H h I i J j K k L l M m N n O o P p Q q R r
S s T t U u V v W w X x Y y Z z

This is roughly ASCII, but the full stop is out of place. This order may vary on non-UK machines.

CHAPTER 8
Extending SuperBASIC

SuperBASIC is the only job running in the QL on switch-on, and is treated specially by QDOS. To distinguish it from other jobs, it has an exclusive job ID of $00000000, and its job header is not in TRNSP, but below it. SuperBASIC is also different in that its data area is not fixed and can expand or contract dynamically. As it lies below TRNSP and RESPR, both of which can expand and contract, it is liable to move around in memory at any time, and for this reason the base of the entire area is always addressed by A6, which is liable to change value at any time. The rest of the data area, including SuperBASIC's system variables and program area, is always referenced relative to A6, and the values of all the pointers are also relative to A6. In addition, the user stack (A7) is also liable to move around at any time, but is 'invisible' to programs. However, it does mean that neither A6 nor A7 should have their values stored anywhere. If you want to store an 'error stack pointer', for example, you cannot do this by simply 'MOVE.L A7,ERR_SP', but store it relative to A6, as this will not change, by:

```
MOVE.L      A7,A1
SUB.L       A6,A1           make it relative
MOVE.L      A1,ERR_SP       now store it
```

(Even this is not perfect — it is still possible for A6 to change between the first and second instructions, so to be absolutely safe it's best to enter supervisor mode when doing this sort of thing.) The memory layout is shown in **Figure 8.1**.

Each section of memory has two pointers — one, such as BV.TKBAS, points to the start while the other, such as BV.TKP, points to the current end of the area used. (The stack areas are unusual in that they are 'upside down'.) Each SuperBASIC system variable is covered in Appendix B.

SuperBASIC is almost unique in that it allows easy extension of its commands and functions by well-defined methods. When done properly, this also means that many different extensions can be added one after the other, and remain compatible. The way the SuperBASIC can be extended is possible because of the way in which it stores everything — most of the commands are defined as procedures, which may be either

117

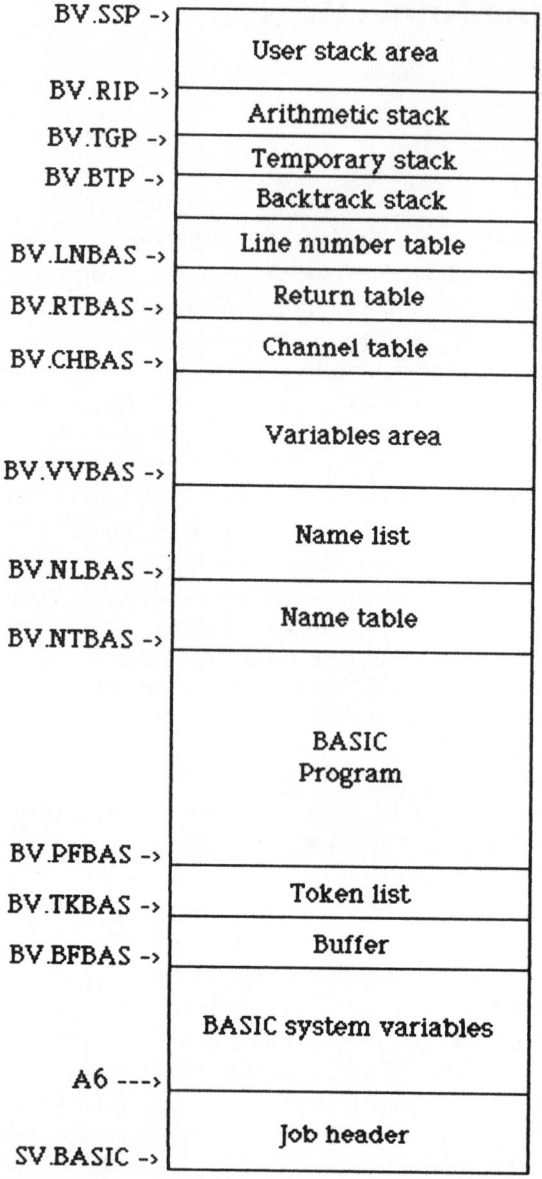

BV.SSP ->

User stack area

BV.RIP ->

Arithmetic stack

BV.TGP ->

Temporary stack

BV.BTP ->

Backtrack stack

BV.LNBAS ->

Line number table

BV.RTBAS ->

Return table

BV.CHBAS ->

Channel table

Variables area

BV.VVBAS ->

Name list

BV.NLBAS ->

Name table

BV.NTBAS ->

BASIC Program

BV.PFBAS ->

Token list

BV.TKBAS ->

BV.BFBAS ->

Buffer

BASIC system variables

A6 --->

Job header

SV.BASIC ->

Figure 8.1:   SuperBASIC Memory Map.

machine code or SuperBASIC (using DEF PROC), as can the functions. (This flexibility does have one unfortunate disadvantage though — the speed with which lines are interpreted.) The keywords that are fixed, and in no way re-definable are:

END, FOR, IF, REPeat, SELect, WHEN ERRor, DEFine, PROCedure, FuNction, GO TO, GO SUB, WHEN EOF, INPUT, RESTORE, NEXT, EXIT, ELSE, ON, RETurn, REMAINDER, DATA, DIM, LOCal, LET, THEN, STEP, REMark, and MISTake

The rest of the keywords are re-definable, functions included, and may be easily added to (see next section). To see how this is possible, it's useful to examine the three main areas associated with this: the name table, the name list, and the variable area.

The name table consists of blocks of eight bytes, which define the ASCII for the name, its type, location and value (where relevant). The format of each entry is:

word   defines the type of the name:

$0001	undefined string variable
$0002	undefined floating point number
$0003	undefined integer
$0101	string expression
$0102	floating point expression
$0103	integer expression
$0201	string variable
$0202	floating point number
$0203	integer
$0300	substring (used internally only)
$0301	string array
$0302	floating point array
$0303	integer array
$0400	SuperBASIC procedure
$0501	SuperBASIC string function
$0502	SuperBASIC floating point function
$0503	SuperBASIC integer function
$0602	REPeat loop name
$0702	FOR loop counter (floating point)
$0800	machine code procedure
$0900	machine code function

word   pointer to entry in name list (or -1 if expression)
long   pointer to 'value'
            For variables this is an offset into the variables area, or if negative then it is undefined.

For SuperBASIC procedures and functions the high word is the line number of the DEF statement.
For machine code functions and definitions the long word is the absolute address of the routine.

The name table lies from BV.NTBAS to BV.NTP (or, put another way, from the areas pointed to by $18(A6) to $1C(A6)).

The 'name list' stores all the ASCII of every name, with a byte defining its length, followed by the ASCII of the name itself. (Note that there are no spare bytes used in this to force them to start on even addresses, unlike most other byte-sized data areas.) It lies from BV.NLBAS to BV.NLP (or $20(A6) to $24(A6)).

The 'variable list' holds the values of all BASIC variables. The form used is:

Strings
These are stored as a word defining the length of the string, followed by the bytes of the string itself. If the string is an odd number of bytes long, it will be internally padded to an even number.

Floating point numbers
These are stored as six bytes, as a 16-bit exponent with a 32-bit mantissa. The format is shown in **Figure 8.2.**

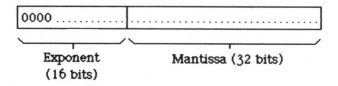

Figure 8.2:   Floating Point Storage.

The exponent is offset by $800+$1F, so the value of the number is mantissa*(2 ↑ (exponent−$81F)). Zero is uniquely represented as six zero bytes.

Integers
Integers are stored as two's-complemented words.

Arrays
These are rather more complex, and start with a long word relative pointer to the actual start of the data. Next, there is a word giving the number of dimensions, then for each dimension there is a pair of words defining the dimension, and the index multiplier for it. After all the dimensions comes the start of the array itself, which will be two bytes per element for integers, six bytes for floating point numbers, or a variable

size for strings. Each string array element is stored in the same way as strings, as described above, again with padding so that the next element always starts on an even address.

Adding procedures and functions

Both additional procedures and functions share certain characteristics, and only really differ when it comes to quit them — with a function, you have to return a value, whereas with a procedure you just return without one. There is a system utility to add procedures and functions to the name list and name table:

BP.INIT — add procedures and functions to BASIC: vector $110

Entry:	A1	start of procedure/function list
	A6	usual SuperBASIC value

Exit:	D1	preserved
	D2	preserved
	D3	corrupted
	A0	preserved
	A1	corrupted
	A2	preserved
	A3	preserved
	A6	may be updated if more memory is required

Errors: none

Action: The procedures and functions defined in a list are added into the system. The list format is:

DC.W PROCNUM   number of procedures

* then for each procedure:
DC.W PROUTINE–*   relative pointer to routine
DC.B PROCLEN   length of procedure name
DC.B 'proc here'   the ASCII of the name

* at end of procedure list
DC.W 0
DC.W FUNCNUM   number of functions

* then for each function
DC.W FROUTINE–*   relative pointer to routine
DC.B FNLEN   length of function name

121

DC.B 'fn here'   the ASCII of the name

* at end of function list

DC.W 0

If your procedures or functions have excessively long names with an average length of over eight characters, the constants PROCNUM and FUNCNUM should each be re-calculated to be:

(total number of procedures or functions+total bytes used in all procedure/function names+7)/8

The routine starts by allocating PROCNUM*8 bytes in both the name table and name list. For each procedure the new name table entry has its first word set to $0800, the second word a relative pointer to the new name list entry, then the length and ASCII bytes are copied into the name list. The long word is then set to the absolute address of the routine, and the process continues until it comes across the $0000 end pointer, when it repeats the process for the function definitions. After calling this, the definition list is not used and may be removed if required.

If you get any parts of the definition list wrong, a system crash is likely. This is because the routine will create erroneously large entries in the name list, which will corrupt whatever follows the name list, until it comes across a $0000 word. By this time the system is usually too corrupted to continue operating normally, so be very careful. In particular, if you are defining, say, procedures only, don't leave off the *two* zero words that will be required (one for the number of functions, the other being the end marker).

The order in which procedures and functions get defined is important — if there is a name clash, the first definition will be the one used. The first entries placed in the list will be any defined by external ROMs, followed by the internal ROM definitions, then any SuperBASIC definitions. For example, if a SuperBASIC procedure called TEST is defined before you try to add in your own machine code TEST procedure, then the Super-BASIC one will be the one used. The only way to remove an entry from the lists is by a New — this clears any SuperBASIC definitions, but not machine code ones. (When an additional command is entered into a line, the case of its name when re-LISTed corresponds to the exact form when defined, or when called if it was undefined.)

Getting parameters

The first thing a procedure or function has to do is get its parameters (or to check that it has none, which is a similar operation). By the time your own routine gets called, SuperBASIC has done a lot of the hard work for you. Each parameter has been copied on to the end of the name table, and in addition certain bits of the type word have been set to show which characters separated the parameters from one another. Register A3 points to the first parameter in the name table, and register A5 points to the last. The format of the low byte of the type word is shown in **Figure 8.3**.

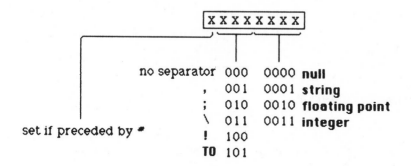

Figure 8.3:   Format of Type Byte for Parameters.

The expression $(A5 - A3)/8$ will give the number of parameters passed. While this information is directly useful for finding parameter types and separators, it would be difficult to extract variable values, were it not for the fact there are some very useful utility routines to do just that. There are four, which evaluate all the parameters in various forms, and put the result on the maths stack. This would be a good place therefore to cover this particular area.

The maths stack

This is an area for storing parameters, both string and numeric, and required when doing any maths operation. In 68008 tradition it is 'upside down' and is illustrated in **Figure 8.4**.

It is conventional to use A1 as the maths stack pointer, and as with all SuperBASIC system variables it must be used relative to A6. Thus, the top item on the stack is at location 0(A6,A1.L), and if it was a floating point number (ie six bytes) then the item underneath it would start at 6(A6,A1.L). (Be wary of the size of A1 in this addressing mode: it must always be long, otherwise the machine may crash — the current ROMs still contain a few word-sized accesses.) On entry to the procedure or function, A1 is a suitable value for the top of the stack.

Word integers take two bytes, long words four bytes, floating point numbers six bytes, and strings take 2+length (or 3+length if odd) bytes.

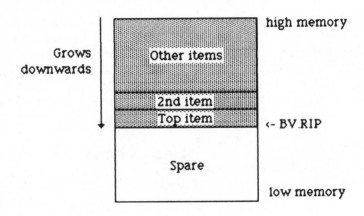

Figure 8.4:   Maths Stack.

If you want to use the stack, perhaps for some calculation, you should check that there is enough room on it, and this is done with a system utility:

BV.CHRIX — reserve space on maths stack: vector $11A

Entry: D1.L   number of bytes required

Exit: D1   corrupted
            D2   corrupted
            D3   corrupted
            A0   preserved
            A1   preserved
            A2   preserved
            A3   preserved

Errors: none

Action: The maths stack is tested to see if there is sufficient extra space for the user's needs — if not, it is expanded. As this can move the stack, the code to use this normally looks something like:

```
MOVE.L      A1,BV.RIP(A6)          store current value
MOVE.W      $11A,A0
JSR         (A0)                   get some space
MOVE.L      BV.RIP(A6),A1          new stack position possibly
```

Get parameters on to maths stack: vectors:
CA.GTINT — $112: get word integers

CA.GTFP — $114: get floating point numbers
CA.GTSTR — $116: get strings
CA.GTLIN — $118: get long integers

Entry:	A1.L	top of maths stack
	A3.L	pointer to first parameter
	A5.L	pointer to last parameter

Exit:	D1	corrupted
	D2	corrupted
	D3.W	number of parameters found
	D4	corrupted
	D6	corrupted
	A0	corrupted
	A1	update pointer to top of stack
	A2	corrupted
	A3	preserved
	A4	preserved
	A5	preserved

Errors:	−15	bad parameter
	−17	error in expression

Action: This evaluates all the parameters from (A3) to (A5) in the specified form, and places the results on the maths stack in the order in which they are found. Thus the first parameter will be on the bottom of the stack, and the last one on the top. Note that the entries in the name table defining the separators can be corrupted by this routine.

As this evaluates all the parameters of the same type, if you wish to evaluate different types then save A5, then set it to A3+8, and you can check the separators before evaluating them individually.

These utilities do not support 'coercion', that is the conversion of variable types. In particular, device names have to be expressed within quotes, so that a line like 'cat mdv2_' will produce an error if string evaluation is attempted — the line needs to be 'cat 'mdv2_' ' to be accepted. Coercion is possible, though (as the inbuilt procedures such as DIR support it), but the relevant routines are not vectored. One can only hope that the next release of the ROM will include the vectors, as this is a lot of code to write yourself.

After evaluating the necessary parameters the required action can be taken, but for an error-free return the maths stack pointer BV.RIP ($58(A6)) must be restored to its value on entry. As is usual with QDOS routines, D0.L should return an error code, or 0 for no error. In the event of an error return the system will 'clean up' the maths stack.

Returning values

All that has been said above is relevant to both procedures and functions, but when it comes to 'return time' functions differ. The value to return from the function has to be the only thing on the maths stack and a key in D4 to tell the system what sort the value is:

1 string
2 floating point
3 word integer

(Unfortunately long words have to be converted to floating point before return.)

If instead of returning a function value you want to return a change in a parameter value, you should put the new value on the maths stack (of the correct type), then use the following system call. This can be used for procedures as well as functions.

BP.LET — return a changed parameter: vector $120

Entry: A3.L   pointer to name table entry of parameter

Exit: D1   corrupted
           D2   corrupted
           D3   corrupted
           A0   corrupted
           A1   corrupted
           A2   corrupted
           A3   preserved

Errors: −15   bad parameter

Action: Before calling this, BV.RIP should be set to point to the top of the stack. Using the element in the name table, the parameter is updated to suit the value on the maths stack.

SuperBASIC channels

SuperBASIC programs have a number of channels associated with them, denoted by a # followed by a number, starting from #0. After a switch-on, three channels are defined — #0 is the input window at the bottom of the screen, and #1 and #2 are the two windows in the rest of the screen. To QDOS, these channels have IDs $00000000, $00010001 and $00020002 respectively, but if they are changed from SuperBASIC then the IDs will change. To keep track of all this SuperBASIC has its own channel table, from BV.CHBAS to BV.CHP ($30(A6) to $34(A6)), which is in the form of 28 bytes for each channel:

0	CH.ID	long	QDOS channel ID (-1 if closed)
4	CH.CCPY	f.p.	current graphics y coordinate
$0A	CH.CCPX	f.p.	current graphics x coordinate
$10	CH.ANGLE	f.p.	turtle angle
$16	CH.PEN	byte	pen position: 0 up, 1 down
$20	CH.CHPOS	word	cursor position across line
$22	CH.WIDTH	word	number of characters per line
$24	CH.SPARE	long	currently unused
$28	CH.LENCH		end of channel block

For non-graphics channels, the turtle graphics parameters have no meaning. CH.WIDTH is initialised to 80 by the Open procedure, and can be changed with the WIDTH command, but is currently otherwise unused. In addition, CH.CHPOS is never referred to at all, so it would seem that these are both present to allow the TAB parameter to be used in PRINT statements, and may be implemented in the future.

Given a channel number, the relevant details can be calculated with the following small routine, which actually lies in the ROM but is not currently vectored:

```
* enter with channel number in D0
DOCHAN    MOVE.L          BV.CHBAS(A6),A0    start of table
          MULU            #$28,D0
          ADD.L           D0,A0              relevant entry
          CMP.L           BV.CHP(A6),A0
          BGE.S           CHNOTF             if it's not in table
          MOVE.L          0(A6,A0.L),D0      channel ID
          BLT.S           CHNOTF             if it's closed
          MOVE.L          A0,A2              BASIC channel area
          MOVE.L          D0,A0              channel ID
          MOVEQ           #0,D0              no error
          RTS
CHNOTF    MOVEQ           #-6,D0             'channel not found'
          RTS
* if channel found:
*         D0=0
*         A0=channel ID
*         A2=BASIC channel table entry (relative A6)
* if channel not found:
          D0=-6
```

When doing I/O operations from SuperBASIC, you have to be aware that all addresses are relative to A6. To help with this, there is a system trap that converts addresses from their relative form into the absolute form that the I/O routines require:

127

BP.ABSIO — convert relative addresses: TRAP #4

Entry: none

Exit: none

Errors: none

Action: This trap should be done prior to a trap #2 or #3 from the BASIC interpreter which requires an address to be passed to it, that would otherwise be relative to A6. It corrupts nothing but D0.

What this does is set bit 7 of JB.RELA6 of the current job. It should thus really never be used from any other job. When the next trap #3 is issued, A6 is added by the IOSS to A0, or alternatively when the next trap #3 is issued, A6 is added to A1. The effect is cancelled when the trap finishes, unless the error 'invalid channel ID' occurs after a trap #3. To cancel it in this case, do:

MOVE.L	$28064,A3	current job
MOVE.L	(A3),A3	find header start
BCLR	#7,$16(A3)	clear the bit

Some examples

This theory is all well and good, but like most things it is best illustrated by example, so here are a couple. The first is a procedure, called CAT, which simplifies the directory command. To use it, enter a line such as 'CAT 1' which is equivalent to the rather unwieldy 'DIR MDV1_'. As well as illustrating the principles behind extending SuperBASIC, it shows how to read directories. After defining a drive number, a CAT on its own will use the same drive, until changed.

Program 8.1: CAT Procedure

```
            MOVE.W $110,A0
            LEA PROCS(PC),A1      link in procedure
            JSR (A0)
            RTS
PROCS:  DC.W 1                    number of procs
            DC.W CAT-*            relative location
            DC.B 3,'CAT'          procedure name
            DC.W 0                end of procs
            DC.W 0                number of fns
            DC.W 0                end of fns

* the procedure itself

CAT     MOVE.W $112,A0
            JSR (A0)              get integers
```

```
            TST.L D0                    error?
            BNE QCAT                    quit if there is
            LEA MDNAME(PC),A0
            CMP.W #1,D3                 number of parameters?
            BGT BADPS                   error as too many
            BNE.S DEFAULT               if none then default
            MOVE.W 0(A6,A1.L),D1        get number off stack
            ADDQ.L #2,$58(A6)           restore maths stack
            CMP.W #9,D1                 check range
            BCC BADPS                   error if too big
            ADD.B #'0',D1               else make into ASCII
            MOVE.B D1,5(A0)             store new drive number
DEFAULT     MOVEQ #-1,D1               'current' job
            MOVEQ #4,D3
            MOVEQ #1,D0
            TRAP #2                     open directory
            TST.L D0                    error?
            BNE QCAT                    if there is then quit
            MOVE.L A0,A5                mdv ID into A5
            MOVE.L #$00010001,A4        output ID in A4
            MOVEQ #$45,D0
            MOVE.L (A6),A1              basic buffer
            BSR.S DOTRP3                get medium details
            BNE.S EXCAT                 if error then close & quit
            MOVE.L D1,-(A7)             save sector nos
            MOVE.L (A6),A1              buffer start
            MOVEQ #$0A,D2               length of name
            BSR.S PRTSTR                print name
            MOVEQ #5,D0
            MOVEQ #10,D1
            TRAP #3                     print LF
            MOVEM.W (A7)+,D1-D2         restore sector count
            MOVE.W D2,D4
            BSR.S PRTNUM                print 1st number
            MOVEQ #5,D0
            MOVE.B #'7',D1              print "/"
            TRAP #3
            MOVE.W D4,D1
            BSR.S PRTNUM                print 2nd number
            MOVEQ #5,D0
            MOVEQ #10,D1
            TRAP #3                     print LF
NXNAME      MOVEQ #3,D0
            MOVEQ #64,D2               number of bytes to get
            MOVE.L (A6),A1
            MOVE.L A5,A0               mdv ID
            MOVEQ #0,D4
            BSR DOTRP3
            BNE Q2                     quit with no error if EOF
            SUB.W #48,A1              start of name
            MOVE.W -2(A6,A1.L),D2     name length
            BEQ.S NXNAME             if null name
            BSR.S PRTSTR             else print the name
            MOVEQ #5,D0
            MOVEQ #10,D1
            TRAP #3                  print LF
            BRA NXNAME               and get next

* Print D1 (word) in decimal

PRTNUM      MOVE.L (A6),A1
            LEA 2(A1),A0
            MOVE.W D1,0(A6,A1.L)     store on stack
            MOVE.W $F2,A2
            JSR (A2)                 convert to ASCII
            MOVE.W D1,D2             length of number - now print it

PRTSTR      MOVEQ #7,D0
            MOVE.L A4,A0             print on screen
DOTRP3      TRAP #4                 make it absolute
            MOVEQ #-1,D3            infinite timeout
            TRAP #3                 do the I/O
            TST.L D0                test for error
```

```
            RTS
EXCAT   MOVE.L  D0,D4           save any error code
Q2      MOVEQ   #2,D0
        TRAP    #2              close the mdv channel
        MOVE.L  D4,D0           restore error
QCAT    RTS                     and quit
BADPS   MOVEQ   #-15,D0         'bad parameter'
        RTS                     quit

* the device filename

MDNAME  DC.W 5                  length
        DC.B  'MDV1_'           the default name
```

The next example is of a new function called QDOS$. It is a complement
to the inbuilt VER$, which gives the SuperBASIC version, and returns a
result like '1.03', using the system trap MT.INF.

Program 8.2: QDOS$ Function

```
        LEA DEFTAB(PC),A1
        MOVE.W  $110,A2
        JSR (A2)                link in function
        RTS

DEFTAB  DC.W 0                  no procedures
        DC.W 0                  end marker for procs
        DC.W 1                  number of functions
        DC.W QDOS-*             pointer
        DC.B 5,'QDOS$'          the function name
        DC.W 0                  end marker for fns

* the function itself

QDOS    MOVEQ   #6,D1           6 bytes required
        MOVE.W  $11A,A4
        JSR (A4)                so check maths stack
        MOVE.L  $58(A6),A1
        SUBQ.W  #4,A1
        MOVEQ   #0,D0
        TRAP    #1              get system info
        MOVE.W  #4,0(A6,A1.L)   store the length word
        MOVE.L  D2,2(A6,A1.L)   followed by the ASCII
        MOVEQ   #1,D4           'string result'
        MOVEQ   #0,D0           no error
        MOVE.L  A1,$58(A6)      update maths stack
        RTS
```

The $ following the name is purely a matter of taste, and machine code
functions, unlike SuperBASIC ones, do not require a character denoting
their type. Like other functions, you cannot directly slice QDOS$ in cur-
rent versions of SuperBASIC, so if you wish to extract the first digit, a
variable has to be used, eg:

A$=QDOS$: PRINT A$(1)

Correcting the CALL bug

In current versions of the ROM there is an error in the CALL procedure which can crash the machine if more than about 25K of SuperBASIC is present and a CALL issued. With other BASICS, such a problem would remain, but thanks to the name table it is possible to re-define the procedure start address to point to a corrected version of it. To do this, the tables have to be searched to find CALL in the name list, and then its entry in the name table.

Program 8.3: Correction of the CALL Bug

```
BV.NTBAS EQU $18
BV.NTP   EQU $1C
BV.NLBAS EQU $20
BV.RIP   EQU $58

* find it first

        MOVE.L BV.NTBAS(A6),A0    start of name table
LOOP    MOVE.W 2(A6,A0.L),A1      name list displacement
        ADDA.L BV.NLBAS(A6),A1
        CMPI.B #4,0(A6,A1.W)      is the name 4 long?
        BEQ COODBE                could be
NEXT    ADDQ.L #8,A0              next name table entry
        CMPA.L BV.NTP(A6),A0
        BLS.S LOOP                if still more
        MOVEQ #-7,D0             else 'not found'
        RTS
COODBE  CMPI.B #'C',1(A6,A1.W)
        BNE NEXT
        CMPI.B #'A',2(A6,A1.W)
        BNE NEXT
        CMPI.B #'L',3(A6,A1.W)
        BNE NEXT
        CMPI.B #'L',4(A6,A1.W)
        BNE NEXT                 check each name byte

* must be the one

        LEA NEWCALL(PC),A2
        MOVE.L A2,4(A6,A0.L)      update the pointer
        CLR.L D0                 no error
        RTS                      return

* new CALL procedure

NEWCALL MOVE.W $118,A4
        JSR (A4)                 get long word parameters
        BNE.S                    exit if error
        LSL.L #2,D3
        BEQ.S BADPARAM           if no parameters
        ADD.L D3,BV.RIP(A6)      restore stack
        MOVE.L 0(A6,A1.L),-(A7)  put start address on stack
        MOVEM.L 4(A6,A1.L),A0-A5/D1-D7  set register values
BADPARAM MOVEQ #-15,D0
EXIT    RTS                      go to it (or return after error)
```

The new CALL procedure is much the same as the old, except that the addressing mode used is long-sized and not word-sized, as in ROM. When the bug does get fixed, this patch will still work but will be redundant.

The method used to find CALL could well be made into a more general routine to find any procedure or function, for re-definition if required.

131

Floating point routines

The QL ROM includes a complete arithmetic package which can be accessed by two different vectors, one for single operations, the other for a sequence. They are very efficient indeed, resulting in exceptionally fast execution times. The package operates using either parameters to and from the maths stack, or a 'variables' area. As it is intended for use in SuperBASIC functions and procedures, the data areas are referenced relative to A6, but other jobs can also use the package either by subtracting A6 from the values of A1 and A4 or, more simply, by zeroing A6. The two entry points to the package are:

Execute maths operation(s): vectors:
RI.EXEC — $11C: one operation
RI.EXECB — $11E: list of operations

Entry:	D0.W	operation code (RI.EXEC only)
	D7.L	should be 0 for reliable operation
	A1.L	pointer to maths stack (relative to A6)
	A3.L	pointer to operations list (RI.EXECB only)
	A4.L	pointer to base of variable area (relative to A6)

Exit:	D1	preserved
	D2	preserved
	D3	preserved
	A0	preserved
	A1	updated pointer to maths stack
	A2	preserved
	A3	preserved
	A4	preserved

Errors:	−18	arithmetic overflow

Action: To do a single operation, use RI.EXEC with D1.W containing the operation code, or to do a sequence of operations then (A3) should point to a list of *bytes* of the codes, ending in a zero. The operation code falls into three ranges — from 2 to $30 inclusive it defines one of the following operations:

OPCODE	NAME	FUNCTION
2	RI.NINT	INT floating point form into word integer
4	RI.INT	truncate floating point form into word integer
6	RI.NLINT	INT floating point form into long integer
8	RI.LINT	convert integer word into floating point form
$0A	RI.ADD	add TOS to NOS
$0C	RI.SUB	subtract TOS from NOS

$0E	RI.MULT	multiply TOS by NOS
$10	RI.DIV	divide TOS into NOS
$12	RI.ABS	take positive value
$14	RI.NEG	negate
$16	RI.DUP	duplicate
$18	RI.COS	cosine
$1A	RI.SIN	sine
$1C	RI.TAN	tangent
$1E	RI.COT	cotangent
$20	RI.ASIN	arcsine
$22	RI.ACOS	arccosine
$24	RI.ATAN	arctangent
$26	RI.ACOT	arccotangent
$28	RI.SQRT	square root
$2A	RI.LN	natural logs
$2C	RI.LOG10	base 10 logs
$2E	RI.EXP	exponential
$30	RI.POWFP	take NOS ↑ TOS

The first four convert between word, long words and floating point forms, with one form being removed from the stack, acted upon, and then replaced in another form. All other operations act exclusively on floating point forms of numbers.

The next four and RI.POWFP use two values from the stack, the top of stack (TOS) and next on stack (NOS), act upon them both, and then return a single result, with the net effect of decreasing the stack by six bytes.

The function RI.DUP duplicates the current item on the top of the stack, and is the only one actually to increase the number of items on it.

The remaining functions all remove the top item, act on it, and replace it with a new value, with no net effect on the maths stack pointer.

As well as the maths stack, the programmer can use a 'variables' area for storing numbers, useful for intermediate results. This area should be pointed to by A4 (relative to A6), and there are two sets of other operation codes for storing and retrieving numbers from the area. To read a number from the area, opcodes with values from $32 to $FE (which must be even) are used. The code is taken as the displacement from A4, giving a range from $-206(A6,A4.L)$ to $-2(A6,A4.L)$. The six-byte floating point number is read from the location specified, and placed on top of the maths stack (so A1 decreases by 6). To store a number in the area, opcodes with odd values from $31 to $FF are used, again taken as relative to A4, though forced to be even (by clearing bit 0), giving the same range as the 'read' function above. The six-byte floating point number is removed from the maths stack and stored in the calculated 'variables' area.

When using the store and retrieve functions from RI.EXEC, the state of bits 8 through 15 of D0 on entry are actually irrelevant, but they are

133

very important when doing codes 2 to $30 — if bits 8–15 are not all zero, the routine will probably crash, so it's best always to pass D0 as a word parameter.

Probably the most often-used part of the floating point package is converting from a register value into a floating point form, to use the graphics I/O traps detailed in Chapter 5. To do this, RI.FLOAT should be used, with code such as this:

```
* put D1.W on to maths stack then convert to floating point form
* assumes A1 points to suitable area (relative A6)
MOVE.W      D1,0(A6,A1.L)      store on stack
MOVEQ       #8,D0              RI.FLOAT
MOVEQ       #0,D7              get ready
MOVE.W      $11C,A0
JSR         (A0)               call the package
* now 0(A6,A1.L) is the f.p. value of D1
```

SuperBASIC memory allocation

There are two system traps for allocating and releasing memory for the SuperBASIC system, but use these with caution, as they are normally used only within SuperBASIC itself, and the user stack pointer can get changed!

MT.ALBAS — allocate BASIC memory area: TRAP #1 with D0=$16

| *Entry:* | D1.L | length of area required |
| | A6.L | usual SuperBASIC pointer |

Exit:	D1.L	length of area allocated
	D2	corrupted
	D3	corrupted
	A0	corrupted
	A1	corrupted
	A2	corrupted
	A3	corrupted
	A6	updated SuperBASIC pointer
	A7	new user stack pointer

| *Errors:* | −3 | out of memory |

Action: An attempt will be made to expand the SuperBASIC area, to the nearest multiple of 16 bytes.

MT.REBAS — release BASIC memory area: TRAP #1 with D0=$17

| *Entry:* | D1.L | number of bytes to release |
| | A6.L | usual SuperBASIC pointer |

Exit:	D1.L	number of bytes released
	D2	corrupted
	D3	corrupted
	A0	corrupted
	A1	corrupted
	A2	corrupted
	A3	corrupted
	A6	updated SuperBASIC pointer
	A7	new user stack pointer

| *Errors:* | none |

CHAPTER 9
External ROMs and Device Drivers

The QL hardware and firmware has been designed for expansion with additional hardware, in the form of external ROMs which may also include extra hardware for peripherals. All extra ROMs have a defined format, so that the QL can recognise them and take action on finding them. There are two areas in which additional ROMs can lie — in the ROM socket at $0C000, or in a peripheral ROM from $C0000 to $FC000 in 16K blocks.

The ROM socket
This can accommodate up to 16K of ROM, and plugs in via the socket on the back of the QL. In the address map it always lies from $0C000 to $0FFFF, and is thus the only place in the memory map that user-written routines can be position dependent.

The peripheral ROMs
Up to 16 peripheral ROMs of 16K each can be added to the QL, though if more than one is added then an additional board, such as the expansion module, is required. As such ROMs can lie anywhere within the memory map, all code within them has to be position independent. They connect via the expansion bus on the left of the QL and can contain ROM, RAM or any other I/O devices, though they must start with ROM for the system to recognise them.

ROM header format
To tell if a ROM is connected or not, the system looks for a specific pattern in it, thus:

```
START   DC.L    $4AFB0001           identification word
        DC.W    BASPROCS–START      start of procedure/function definitions (or 0)
        DC.W    INIT–START          initialisation routine (or 0)
        DC.W    NAMELEN             length of ROM name
        DC.B    "ROM name",10       the name itself+LF
```

BASPROCS should be a list of SuperBASIC procedures and functions to be added to the system, in the same form as described in the previous chapter, or 0 if there are none to be added. INIT should point to the initialisation routine called after power-up, or 0 if one is not required. The INIT routine will be executed in user mode, and if a successful return to QDOS is required then registers A0 (zero), A3 (points to the start of the ROM) and A6 ($28000) should not be altered. When INIT is called, the system tables and BASIC have been set up, but channel 0 is the only channel open. Other channels should *not* be opened by the INIT routine. Channel 0 is initially the top section of the screen, and all ROM names found are printed in it. For this reason, they should not be longer than 36 characters and should end in a LF character.

Peripheral ROM problem

While this method is a very neat way of adding ROMs to the QL, there is a problem with peripheral ROMs — in QDOS 1.03 and earlier, there is an error in the 'look for peripherals' routine that terminates the search after checking for one device driver only, so other peripherals are ignored. One way to get around this is for the INIT routine in every peripheral to see if the peripheral is the first, and if it is then it has to carry on the search as the ROM should. This is complicated by the fact that the patch to fix it has to work once the ROM gets corrected. Thus the INIT routine has to look something like this:

```
INIT     BSR       NORMINIT          call the INIT routine
         CMP.L     #$C0000,A3        is it the first?
         BEQ.S     NEXT              if so
         RTS                         it isn't so quit
NEXT     ADD.L     #$4000,A3         try next one
         CMP.L     #$100000,A3       at the end?
         BGE.S     NOMORE            if so
```

```
* it might be a ROM so let's see
         CMP.L     #$4AFB0001,(A3)
         BNE       NEXT              no so do next
         LEA       8(A3),A1          start of name
         MOVE.W    UT.MTEXT,A2
         JSR       (A2)              print the name
         MOVE.W    4(A3),D0          BASIC procedures and functions
         BEQ.S     NOBAS
         LEA       0(A3,D0.W),A1
         MOVE.W    BP.INIT,A2
         JSR       (A2)              add the procedures and functions
NOBAS    MOVE.W    6(A3),D0          INIT routine
         BEQ.S     NEXT              if none
         JSR       0(A3,D0.W)        call the INIT routine
         BEQ       NEXT              get next ROM
```

```
* here when all have been done
NOMORE  ADDQ.L    #4,A7           remove return address
        ADD.L     #$1E,(A7)       skip over rest of routine
        RTS                       and go back to it
```

This fix assumes that the number of bytes taken by the erroneous routine will remain constant from ROM to ROM. If all device drivers take similar action to the above, then there will be no need to fix the bugs anyway, and the number of bytes will remain constant.

Note that, unlike the usual use of BP.INIT, ROM procedures and functions get added *before* the built-in ones, so if there is a name clash then the external ROM version will override the usual built-in ones.

Device drivers

One of the uses for external ROMs is no doubt that of adding device drivers to the system. It is also possible to add RAM-based device drivers, which is actually easier in some aspects.

Simple device drivers

These are much more straightforward than directory drivers, though they share certain features. Simple drivers consist of several parts — the driver itself is usually in two parts: the access layer, which is called by the IOSS and looks after the I/O traps, opening and closing them; and possibly a physical layer, called from an interrupt, which does the actual transferring of bytes from buffers to the device. When the driver is installed, a device driver linkage block may be set up (a section of RAM for storing information for the driver), and a channel definition block will be set up for every open channel.

Linking a device driver

A linked list is maintained for device drivers, with a pointer SV.DRLST to its start. Devices are added to the start of the list, and in the event of a name clash will override the usual devices. It is suggested that each driver creates an area of RAM in the common heap for its driver linkage block, which should be at least 24 long words in length. This is not obligatory and in fact none of the standard device drivers use linkage blocks. If you choose to have one, it is always addressed relative to A3 and should follow this defined format:

0(A3)   link to next external interrupt link
4(A3)   address of external interrupt
8(A3)   link to next polled interrupt link

$0C(A3)$	address of polled interrupt
$10(A3)$	link to next scheduler interrupt link
$14(A3)$	address of scheduler interrupt
$18(A3)$	link to next device driver
$1C(A3)$	address of I/O routine
$20(A3)$	address of channel open routine
$24(A3)$	address of channel close routine
$28(A3)$	free to use for whatever purpose

If you do not have a driver linkage block, you must have a block of four long words in RAM anyway, to form the link and address for the driver itself. The form of the block *must* be:

```
DC.L      0                     used for link to next one
DC.L      DEV_IO                I/O routine
DC.L      DEV_OPEN              open routine
DC.L      DEV_CLOSE             close routine
```

As code has to be position independent, this table has to be set up with lines such as:

```
LEA       LINK(PC),A0           start of block
LEA       DEV_IO(PC),A1
MOVE.L    A1,4(A0)
LEA       DEV_OPEN(PC),A1
MOVE.L    A1,8(A0)
etc
```

Once either type of block has been set up, it has to be linked into the system, which is done using a system trap:

MT.LIOD — link device driver into list: TRAP #1 with D0=$20

Entry: A0.L   address of link

Exit: D1   preserved
            D2   preserved
            D3   preserved
            A0   preserved
            A1   corrupted
            A2   preserved
            A3   preserved

Errors: none

Action: The block of four long words in RAM is linked into the beginning of the device driver list, defined by SV.DRLST.

If you have a driver linkage block in the standard format, then an 'LEA $18(A3),A0' will set up the register ready to call MT.LIOD. Similar LEAs can be used for linking the interrupts routines conveniently, too.

MT.RIOD — unlink a deviced driver: TRAP #1 with D0=$21

Entry: A0.L   address of link

Exit:	D1	preserved
	D2	preserved
	D3	preserved
	A0	preserved
	A1	corrupted
	A2	preserved
	A3	preserved

Errors: none

Action: The link is removed from the device driver linked list.

Access layer
There are three parts to the access layer, and all are called from the IOSS in supervisor mode — Open, Close, and I/O.

Channel open
On entry, the registers set by the IOSS are:

D3	open type (usually)
A0	start of device name (word of length followed by ASCII)
A3	assumed start of driver definition block
A6	system variables (=$28000)

An open routine must first check the name, to see if it corresponds to the device, and there is a useful system vector to do this:

IO.NAME — decode device name: vector $122

Entry:	A0.L	start of name
	A3.L	pointer to parameter block for results

Exit:	D1	corrupted
	D2	corrupted
	D3	corrupted
	A0	preserved
	A1	corrupted
	A2	corrupted
	A3	preserved

Errors:	−7	device not found
	−12	bad device name — recognised but bad parameters

Action: This decodes the device name and evaluates its parameters in a buffer. Following the JSR, there should be three short branches, followed by the data for the device decoding. The first branch will be taken if the name was 'not found', the second if it was a 'bad device name', and the third if it was OK. The data for the device name has to follow a fixed format, giving this general layout:

MOVE.W	IO.NAME,A1	
JSR	(A1)	decode it
BRA.S	NOTIT	if not found
BRA.S	BADPS	if bad parameters
BRA.S	NAMEOK	if it was OK
DC.W	NAMLEN	length of device name
DC.B	'dev name'	ASCII of name (in upper case)
DC.W	NUMPAR	number of parameters following name

* and for every parameter		
DC.W	'_',DEF	space, separator then default

* or		
DC.W	−1,DEFAULT	negative number then default value

* or		
DC.B	NUMPS,'params'	number of possible characters, then the characters
*		themselves

Note that all word data *must* be aligned on word boundaries. Some examples may illustrate the parameter forms more clearly:

The NET description is:

DC.W	3,'NET'	the name
DC.W	2	number of parameters
DC.W	2,'OI'	direction: either O or I
DC.W	'_',0	space, underscore then default station number

The SER description is:

DC.W	3,'SER'	the name
DC.W	4	number of parameters
DC.W	−1,1	port number: default=1
DC.W	4,'OEMS'	possible parity
DC.W	2,'IH'	handshake or ignore
DC.W	3,'RZC'	raw, CTRL Z or continuous

The SCR description is:

DC.W	3,'CON'	the name
DC.W	4	number of parameters
DC.W	' _',448	width: default=448
DC.W	' _',180	depth: default=180
DC.W	' X',32	x origin: default=32
DC.W	' A',16	y origin: default=16

The parameters, or their default values if not present, are stored as words in the buffer area starting at (A3) in the order in which the name is scanned. A useful place for this buffer is on the stack and, for example, the way the SCR open routine creates its buffer is by:

SUB.L	#8,A7	make room for 4 words
MOVE.L	A7,A3	the buffer start

but if you do this be sure you restore the stack before exiting, by doing for example:

ADD.L	#8,A7

The words placed in the buffer correspond to either the value of the parameter, if it is numeric, or a number corresponding to the position of the item in the list of characters.

Having decoded the name, an RTS should be made if the device name was not as it should have been. If the device name was right, the next thing to do is to allocate some common heap space for the channel definition block, and this should be done using MM.ALCHP, and not MT.ALCHP. If an 'out of memory' error occurs after this call then an exit should be made from the routine. If not, then the channel definition block should have its contents set to suit the driver, which should include the values of any parameters worked out by IO.NAME. On return from a successful Open, the IOSS is responsible for setting CH.LEN, CH.DRIVR, CH.OWNER, CH.RFLAG, CH.TAG, CH.STAT, CH.ACTN and CH.JOBWT, and for this reason the start of the channel definition block must be returned in A0. The IOSS also deals with setting up the channel table. For any unsuccessful Open, register A0 *must* be preserved.

Channel close

On entry, the registers are:

A0   start of channel definition block
A3   assumed start of device definition block
A6   system variables = $28000

The routine should clear up any remaining buffers, then reclaim the area using MM.RECHP, not MT.RECHP. The IOSS is responsible for clearing up the channel table. It is normal for no errors to be returned from this routine, as most software assumes this to be the case.

Channel I/O

On entry to this the registers are:

D0.B   operation type (IOSS clears top three bytes)
D1   parameter (usually — see below)
D2   parameter
D3   0 if first entry, or =1 if subsequent call was not complete
A0   start of channel definition block
A1   parameter
A2   parameter
A3   assumed start of driver definition
A6   system variables (=$28000)

In addition, for string operations D1 is set to 0 by the IOSS on the first call. Registers D2–D7/A2–A5 can be used as required by the driver, and A1 and D1 can be set on exit for convenience on re-entry if 'not complete'.

Queue handling

There is a standard way of implementing queues under QDOS, and a number of routines exist to aid in their use. Queues require four long words for pointers, followed by the actual bytes of the queue. The format is:

0	Q.NEXTQ	long	link to next queue, and bit 31 used to mark 'EOF'
4	Q.END	long	pointer to physical end of queue
8	Q.NEXTIN	long	pointer to location to put next byte into (back of queue)
$0C	Q.NXTOUT	long	pointer to location to take next byte from (front of queue)
$10	Q.QUEUE		physical start of queue

The first word only has bit 31 used by the routines, the rest can be used by software for linking to other lists, which is indeed done by the system keyboard queue.

IO.QSET — set up a queue: vector $DC

| *Entry:* | D1.L | queue length |
| | A2.L | location of queue header |

Exit:	D1	preserved
	D2	preserved
	D3	preserved
	A0	preserved
	A1	preserved
	A2	preserved
	A3	start of actual queue

Errors: none (D0 preserved so ignore value on return)

Action: The queue header is set up to an empty queue, by zeroing Q.NEXTQ, setting Q.END to be Q.QUEUE+D1, and Q.NEXTIN and Q.NXTOUT both to Q.QUEUE+D1−1.

IO.QTEST — test queue status: vector $DE

| *Entry:* | A2.L | location of queue header |

Exit:	D1.B	next byte to be read
	D2.L	free space in queue
	D3	preserved
	A0	preserved
	A1	preserved
	A2	preserved
	A3	Q.NXTOUT

| *Errors:* | −1 | queue is empty |
| | −10 | queue is at EOF |

Action: This tests the status of the queue. Q.NEXTIN is compared with Q.NXTOUT and if they are different then the length of the free space is calculated before returning. If they are the same then the queue is either empty or at EOF, and bit 31 of Q.NEXTQ is tested to see which it is.

145

IO.QIN — place byte in queue: vector $E0

Entry:	D1.B	data
	A 2.L	pointer to queue header

Exit:	D1	preserved
	D2	preserved
	D3	preserved
	A0	preserved
	A1	preserved
	A2	preserved
	A3	corrupted

Errors:	−1	queue is full

Action: This puts a byte into a queue. First its EOF status is examined: if the queue has been marked EOF, nothing is done and no error return is made. Next the size of the queue is tested, and an error return made if the queue is already full. If not, then the byte is stored.

IO.QOUT — read a byte from a queue: vector $E2

Entry:	A2.L	pointer to queue

Exit:	D1.B	byte read
	D2	preserved
	D3	preserved
	A0	preserved
	A1	preserved
	A2	preserved
	A3	corrupted

Errors:	−1	queue is empty
	−10	queue is EOF

Action: An attempt is made to read a byte from the queue, provided it is not empty or at EOF.

IO.QEOF — put EOF marker in queue: vector $E4

Entry:	A2.L	pointer to queue header

Exit:	D1	preserved
	D2	preserved
	D3	preserved
	A0	preserved
	A1	preserved
	A2	preserved
	A3	preserved

Errors: none (D0 preserved by the call)

Action: The queue has its status set to EOF. This actually consists of one instruction, namely TAS (A2).

The 'minimum' device driver need only contain three I/O routines — test for pending input, read a byte, and send a byte. Given these, there is a utility routine that 'converts' these into all the other I/O operations, in the way described in Chapter 4.

IO.SERIO — general I/O: vector $EA

Entry:	D1	IOSS value
	D2	IOSS value
	D3	IOSS value
	A1	IOSS value

Exit:	D1	IOSS value
	D2	IOSS value
	D3	possibly corrupted
	D4	corrupted
	D5	corrupted
	A0	preserved
	A1	IOSS value
	A2	possibly corrupted
	A3	possibly corrupted
	A4	corrupted

Errors:	−5	buffer overflow
	−15	bad parameter if illegal operation
	may be other errors depending on driver

Action: The more complex I/O operations are done using just the three supplied routines. Following the JSR, there should be three long words defining each routine, and control will pass to the instruction following the last word. As code has to be position independent, this is rather tricky for ROM drivers, and the ideal place for it is in the device definition block thus:

```
$28(A3)    MOVE.W    IO.SERIO,A4
           JSR       (A4)           call it
           DC.L      DEV_PEND       pending test
           DC.L      DEV_FETCH      fetch byte
           DC.L      DEV_SEND       send byte
           RTS
```

The actual routines must use D0 as an error code, D1 for passing the value of the byte, and can use D1–D3/A1–A3 as required. A0 will point to the channel definition block, and A6 to the system variables.

If the device driver uses standard format queues for its I/O, with the physical layer doing the actual byte transfer, there is another utility that handles all the I/O operations for you:

IO.SERQ — do queue I/O: vector $E8

Entry:	D1	IOSS value
	D2	IOSS value
	D3	IOSS value
	A1	IOSS value

Exit:	D1	IOSS value
	D2	IOSS value
	D3	preserved
	D4	corrupted
	D5	corrupted
	A0	channel definition block
	A1	IOSS value
	A2	corrupted
	A3	corrupted
	A4	corrupted

Errors:	−5	buffer overflow
	−15	bad parameter if illegal operation

Action: The standard queue handling routines are used for pending, fetch and send, and IO.SERIO is used for the IOSS I/O operations.

For this to work, $18 in the channel definition block points to the input queue header, and $1C must point to the output queue header, with either being zero if there is no queue. Incidentally, this is exactly the action taken for pipe I/O.

Directory device driver

Directory drivers are intended for interfacing mass storage media to QDOS, and are much more complicated than normal device drivers. There is only one directory driver on the standard machine, namely the microdrive. Directory drivers consist of similar sections to normal drivers; namely an access layer used by the IOSS, and probably a physical layer for actually doing the hardware I/O with the device. However, the allocation of RAM is a little different to normal device drivers as more areas are required, and the IOSS is more responsible for the allocation. Directory device names have a fixed format, namely any number of ASCII characters (though a maximum of four is recommended for brevity), followed by an ASCII drive number from 1–8 inclusive, then an underline. The IOSS always checks for such a valid start to a device name. As with normal drivers, it is recommended that a device driver linkage block be set up for each driver, though the inbuilt MDV driver does not use one. The area is addressed by A3, and the standard format is:

0(A3)	link to next external interrupt link
4(A3)	address of external interrupt
8(A3)	link to next polled interrupt link
$0C(A3)	address of polled interrupt
$10(A3)	link to next scheduler interrupt link
$14(A3)	address of scheduler interrupt
$18(A3)	link to next directory device driver
$1C(A3)	address of I/O routine
$20(A3)	address of channel open routine
$24(A3)	address of channel close routine
$28(A3)	address of forced slaving entry
$2C(A3)	reserved for Rename (not yet implemented)
$30(A3)	reserved for Truncate (not yet implemented)
$34(A3)	address of format routine
$38(A3)	length of physical definition block
$3C(A3)	word length of device name (eg MDV) followed by bytes of device name

If you do not have a directory driver linkage block in this format, then you must have a block of at least nine long words, in this form:

DC.L	0	used to link to next one
DC.L	DEV_IO	I/O routine
DC.L	DEV_OPEN	open routine
DC.L	DEV_CLOSE	close routine
DC.L	DEV_SLAVE	forced slaving routine
DC.L	0	reserved for Rename
DC.L	0	reserved

149

DC.L	DEV_FORMAT	format routine
DC.L	DEV_PDLEN	length of physical definition block
DC.W	NAMELEN	word length of device name
DC.B	'name'	ASCII of name itself

As code is normally position independent, it has to be set up with lots of LEA xx(PC) instructions. Once either block has been set up, it has to be linked into the system, which is done using a system trap:

MT.LDD — link in directory device driver: TRAP #1 with D0=$22

Entry: A0.L   address of link

Exit: D1   preserved
          D2   preserved
          D3   preserved
          A0   preserved
          A1   corrupted
          A2   preserved
          A3   preserved

Errors: none

Action: The block of data in RAM is linked into the beginning of the directory device driver list, defined by SV.DDLST.

If you have a linkage block in the standard format, then an LEA $18(A3),A0 will set up the register ready to be linked. Similar LEAs can be used for linking in the interrupt routines.

MT.RDD — unlink a directory driver: TRAP #1 with D0=$23

Entry: A0.L   address of link

Exit: D1   preserved
          D2   preserved
          D3   preserved
          A0   preserved
          A1   corrupted
          A2   preserved
          A3   preserved

Errors: none

Action: The link is removed from the directory list.

Access layer

There are five parts to the access layer, and all are called from the IOSS in supervisor mode — open, close, I/O, forced slaving, and format.

Channel open

This is rather different to normal device drivers — the IOSS checks the name and drive number and, by the time the open routine is called, both the channel definition block and the drive's physical definition block have been created and partly filled. The registers on entry are:

A0   channel definition block
A1   physical definition block for drive
A3   assumed start of linkage block

Note that the open routine does not directly know the type of the Open — this can be read if required from FS.ACCES (at $1C(A0)). For a call to open a shared file, the device's open routine is not called but FS.NBYTE is set to $40 (ie immediately past the header which is the start of the actual file) and FS.EBLOK and FS.EBYTE copied from the first channel open to the same file.

All registers except A0 and A6 may be used, with an error returning in D0.L. If an error does occur, the IOSS is responsible for reclaiming the heap used for the channel definition.

The delete operation should be handled in a similar way, except that the access type is −1. Again the IOSS will reclaim the channel definition on return.

Close and input/output

These routines have similar attributes to those for normal device drivers, though note that neither is passed a register for the drive's physical definition block, though this should not normally be necessary anyway.

Forced slaving

Slave blocks can be used to buffer sector contents via RAM, used extensively by the MDV driver and responsible for the improvement in performance compared to the ZX microdrives. This entry point is used by QDOS as a result of other memory allocating routines that require the use of the slave block so the device driver must physically write it out to the hardware. On entry, the register values are:

A1   offending slave block
A2   physical definition block
A3   device linkage start

Registers D0–D3/A0–A4 may be used as required.
  One problem with using slave blocks in your own device drivers is that the routines for their allocation and reclamation are not vectored, and thus have to be duplicated. The use of slave blocks is a complex affair, and of limited practical use, so will not be covered further.

Format routine
This should format a medium ready for use. On entry, the register values are:

A0   pointer to medium name (including device name)
A3   assumed start of device linkage block

Registers D1–D7/A0–A5 may be used as required, with D0 returning an error code, D1.W the number of good sectors, and D2.W the total number of sectors. As actual hardware I/O is required by this, and definition blocks are not allocated by the IOSS, it is usual for format routines to disable interrupts while the hardware signals are done.

APPENDIX A
Doing Without QDOS

While most of the time programs on the QL run under QDOS, there is one feature that is very difficult to use without doing away with QDOS — the second screen. Normally the screen memory lies from $20000 to $27FFF inclusive, but for some software, such as high-speed animation, the alternate screen location of $28000 to $2FFFF is required. Unfortunately, QDOS cannot support this second screen as its system variables and tables lie in the same area, so to use it the whole of QDOS has to be disabled.

To run without QDOS, the 68008 has to stay in supervisor mode, to prevent the system from entering the scheduler. Next, interrupts should be disabled, with OR.W #$0700,SR, and then the SSP should be set to a suitable value, as it will otherwise lie in the middle of screen 1's memory.

To switch between screen modes, MC.STAT at $18063 should be written to, with bit 7 controlling the displayed picture, bit 3 the screen mode (256 or 512), and bit 1 to turn the display on or off. Note that this is a read only register, so if you wish to know its value you should store a copy of what you write into it somewhere in RAM. With QDOS disabled, none of the I/O traps (#2 or #3) will work, and neither will any job control traps. Those system traps and utilities that will remain working without QDOS are summarised here:

MT.IPCOM	send command to IPC
MT.RCLK	read clock
MT.SCLCK	set clock
MT.ACLCK	adjust clock
UT.LINK	link item into list
UT.UNLNK	unlink an item from list
MM.ALLOC	allocate heap space
MM.LNKFR	link free space into heap
IO.QSET	set up queue header
IO.QTEST	test queue status
IO.QIN	put byte into queue
IO.QOUT	take byte from queue
IO.QEOF	make queue as EOF
UT.CSTR	string comparison

RI.EXEC   do maths operation
RI.EXECB   do several maths operations
MD.READ   read a microdrive sector
MD.WRITE   write a microdrive sector
MD.VERIN   verify a sector
MD.SECTR   read sector header
CN.DATE   get date string
CN.DAY   get day string
as well as all the other CN conversion utilities

Probably the most important of these is the IPC command trap, as this is the only way of scanning the keyboard without QDOS. As none of the I/O traps work, accessing devices has to be done directly.

The serial ports are probably the simplest to access directly for output, using PC.IPCRD at $18020. Bit 1 should be examined first, and will be set if the microdrive buffer within the ULA is full, and no output should be attempted because of timing problems. Next the handshake lines should be checked, if required, namely bit 4 (port 1) and bit 5 (port 2), which will be set if the receiving device is not ready. If it is, then the data can be transmitted by writing the byte into PC.TDATA, at $18022. To switch between ports 1 and 2, bit 3 of PC.TCTRL at $18002 should be toggled.

The microdrives can be controlled using the motor and sector control routines described in Chapter 5, though it's rather hard going using them without QDOS! While motors are on, it's best not to try any other direct I/O operations.

It is unlikely that the Net is required by software running without QDOS, but if it is then the routines lying towards the end of the ROM have to be used for sending and receiving packets, but as they are not currently vectored this calling code will be ROM dependent.

APPENDIX B
QDOS Constants

Error codes

−1	not complete	−11	drive full
−2	invalid job	−12	bad device name
−3	out of memory	−13	Xmit error
−4	out of range	−14	format failed
−5	buffer overflow	−15	bad parameter
−6	channel not open	−16	file error
−7	not found	−17	error in expression
−8	file already exists	−18	arithmetic overflow
−9	in use	−19	not implemented
−10	end of file	−20	read only
		−21	bad line

SuperBASIC variables

0	BV.BFBAS	long	buffer base
4	BV.BFP	long	
8	BV.TKBAS	long	token list
$0C	BV.TKP	long	
$10	BV.PFBAS	long	program file
$14	BV.PFP	long	
$18	BV.NTBAS	long	name table
$1C	BV.NTP	long	
$20	BV.NLBAS	long	name list
$24	BV.NLP	long	
$28	BV.VVBAS	long	variable area
$2C	BV.VVP	long	
$30	BV.CHBAS	long	channel table
$34	BV.CHP	long	
$38	BV.RTBAS	long	return table
$3C	BV.RTP	long	
$40	BV.LNBAS	long	line number table
$44	BV.LNP	long	
$48	BV.BTP	long	backtrack stack used during parsing
$4C	BV.BTBAS	long	
$50	BV.TGP	long	temporary graph stack
$54	BV.TGBAS	long	
$58	BV.RIP	long	maths stack

$5C	BV.RIBAS	long	
$60	BV.SSP	long	system stack
$64	BV.SSBAS	long	
$68	BV.LINUM	word	current line number
$6A	BV.LENGTH	word	current length
$6C	BV.STMNT	byte	current statement
$6D	BV.CONT	byte	0, stop processing; $80, continue processing
$6E	BV.INLIN	byte	processing in-line clause: 0 no; 1 loop; $FF other
$6F	BV.SING	byte	immediate mode: 0 off; $FF on
$70	BV.INDEX	word	name table index
$72	BV.VVFREE	long	first free space in VVTABLE
$76	BV.SSSAV	long	value of SP to go to when memory error occurs
$7A		6 bytes	currently unused
$80	BV.RAND	long	random number
$84	BV.COMCH	long	input channel ID
$88	BV.NXLIN	word	line number to start after
$8A	BV.NXSTM	byte	statement to start after
$8B	BV.COMLN	byte	command line saved ($FF) or not (0)
$8C	BV.STOPN	word	set stop number
$8E	BV.EDIT	byte	edit marker: $FF edited, 0 not
$8F	BV.BRK	byte	break during I/O (0) or not ($80)
$90	BV.UNRVL	byte	unravel ($FF) or not (0)
$91	BV.CNSTM	byte	statement to CONT after
$92	BV.CNLNO	word	line number to CONT after
$94	BV.DALNO	word	current DATA line number
$96	BV.DASTM	byte	current DATA statement number
$97	BV.DAITM	byte	DATA item counter
$98	BV.CNIND	word	loop index to CONT with
$9A	BV.CNINL	byte	loop flag to CONT with
$9B	BV.LSANY	byte	checking list ($FF) or not (0)
$9C	BV.LSBEF	word	invisible top line number
$9E	BV.LSBAS	word	bottom line number in window
$A0	BV.LSAFT	word	invisible bottom line number
$A2	BV.LENLN	word	length of window line
$A4	BV.MAXLN	word	number of lines in window
$A6	BV.TOTLN	word	number of window lines so far (overwritten by trap when changing window)
$A8		word	currently unused
$AA	BV.AUTO	byte	$FF when EDIT or AUTO else 0
$AB	BV.PRINT	byte	print from PRTOK ($FF) or not (0)
$AC	BV.EDLIN	word	next editable line number
$AE	BV.EDINC	word	AUTO increment number
$B0	BV.TKPOS	long	location of A4 in token list when starting PROC
$B4	BV.PTEMP	long	temporary pointer
$B8	BV.UNDO	byte	undo return stack (resulting in 'PROCs/FNs cleared')
$B9	BV.ARROW	byte	arrow down ($FF), up (1) or neither (0)
$BA	BV.LSFIL	word	where to fill window to
$BC		68 bytes	currently unused
$100	BV.END		end of BASIC system variables

System variables

163840	$28000	SV.IDENT	long	identification word $D254
163844	$28004	SV.CHEAP	long	start of common heap
163848	$28008	SV.CHPFR	long	first free space in common heap
163852	$2800C	SV.FREE	long	start of free area
163856	$28010	SV.BASIC	long	start of SuperBASIC area
163860	$28014	SV.TRNSP	long	start of transient program area
163864	$28018	SV.TRNFR	long	first free area in TRNSP
163868	$2801C	SV.RESPR	long	start of resident procedure area
163872	$28020	SV.RAMT	long	end of RAM+1 (=$40000 for 128K)
163876	$28024		10 bytes	unused
163886	$2802E	SV.RAND	word	pseudo-random number
163888	$28030	SV.POLLM	word	number of poll interrupts missed
163890	$28032	SV.TVMOD	byte	0 monitor, <>0 TV (corrupted by MODE command)
163891	$28033	SV.SCRST	byte	0 screen active, <>0 inactive, toggled by pressing CTRL F5
163892	$28034	SV.MCSTA	byte	copy of TV register (MC.STAT)
163893	$28035	SV.PCINT	byte	copy of interrupt register (PC.INTR)
163894	$28036		byte	not used
163895	$28037	SV.NETNR	byte	network station number 1–64 (default=1)
163896	$28038	SV.I2LST	long	start of external interrupt list
163900	$2803C	SV.PLIST	long	start of polled tasks list
163904	$28040	SV.SHLST	long	start of scheduler tasks list
163908	$28044	SV.DRLST	long	start of simple device driver list
163912	$28048	SV.DDLST	long	start of directory driver list
163916	$2804C	SV.KEYQ	long	current keyboard queue (or 0 if none)
163920	$28050	SV.TRAPV	long	current RAM vector table (or 0 if none)
163924	$28054	SV.BTPNT	long	most recent slave block entry
163928	$28058	SV.BTBAS	long	start of slave block table
163932	$2805C	SV.BTTOP	long	end of slave block table
163936	$28060	SV.JBTAG	word	current value of job tag
163938	$28062	SV.JBMAX	word	highest job number to date
163940	$28064	SV.JBPNT	long	current job table entry
163944	$28068	SV.JBBAS	long	start of job table
163948	$2806C	SV.JBTOP	long	end of job table
163952	$28070	SV.CHTAG	word	current value of channel tag
163954	$28072	SV.CHMAX	word	highest channel number to date

163956	$28074	SV.CHPNT	long	last channel checked by the waiting I/O scheduler routine
163960	$28078	SV.CHBAS	long	start of channel table
163964	$2807C	SV.CHTOP	long	end of channel table
163968	$28080		8 bytes	unused
163976	$28088	SV.CAPS	word	caps lock: 0 off, $FF00 on
163978	$2808A	SV.ARBUF	word	last key pressed
163980	$2808C	SV.ARDEL	word	key repeat delay (normally 30)
163982	$2808E	SV.ARFRQ	word	key repeat frequency (normally 4)
163984	$28090	SV.ARCNT	word	key repeat counter
163986	$28092	SV.CQCH	word	change keyboard queue code (normally 3=CTRL C)
163988	$28094	SV.WP	word	should be write protect status of microdrives but not implemented
163990	$28096	SV.SOUND	word	sound status: 0 off, $FF00 on
163992	$28098	SV.SER1C	long	address of serial port 1 input queue
163996	$2809C	SV.SER2C	long	address of serial port 2 input queue
164000	$280A0	SV.TMODE	byte	ULA transmit mode: bits 0–2: baud rate number bit 3: 0 ser1, 1 ser2 bit 4: microdrive turning
164002	$280A2	SV.CSUB	long	routine to call when CAPS LOCK is held down
164006	$280A6	SV.TIMO	word	counter for timing serial output
164008	$280A8	SV.TIMOV	word	value of above timeout (=1200/baud +1)
164010	$280AA	SV.FSTAT	word	cursor flash counter
164012	$280AC		66 bytes	unused
164078	$280EE	SV.MDRUN	byte	currently turning microdrive
164079	$280EF	SV.MDCNT	byte	microdrive counter
164080	$280F0	SV.MDDID	8 bytes	drive ID*4 for every drive
164088	$280F8	SV.MDSTA	8 bytes	status of each drive
164096	$28100	SV.FSDEF	16 long	pointers to physical definitions
164160	$28140	SV.STACB	192 long	lowest position for SSP
164992	$28480	SV.STACT		highest position for SSP

Job header

$00	JB.LEN	long	length of job area (including header)
$04	JB.START	long	start address of the job — set when job created
$08	JB.OWNER	long	the owner of the job (or 0 if independent)
$0C	JB.HOLD	long	location to be cleared when job removed (or 0 if not required)
$10	JB.TAG	word	job tag (ie high word of job ID)
$12	JB.PRIOR	byte	priority

$13	JB.PRINC	byte	priority increment (0 if inactive)
$14	JB.STAT	word	status:
			0: possibly active
			positive: delay time until re-activation
			−1: suspended
			−2: waiting for another job to complete
			(no other negative values allowed)
$16	JB.RELA6	byte	bit 7 set immediately after trap #4
$17	JB.WFLAG	byte	bit 7 set if another job waiting for completion
$18	JB.WJOB	long	ID for above waiting job
$1C	JB.TRAPV	long	RAM exception vector location (0 if none)
$20	JB.D0	long	storage for D0
. . .	. . .	. . .	. . .
$3C	JB.D7	long	storage for D7
$40	JB.A0	long	storage for A0
. . .	. . .	. . .	. . .
$5C	JB.A7	long	storage for A7=USP (not SSP)
$60	JB.SR	word	storage for SR
$62	JB.PC	long	storage for program counter
$66		word	not used
$68	JB.END		start of actual job or data

Channel definition block

$00	CH.LEN	long	length of this definition block
$04	CH.DRIVR	long	pointer to linkage block of device driver
$08	CH.OWNER	long	ID of owner job
$0C	CH.RFLAG	long	location to be set when space released
$10	CH.TAG	word	channel tag
$12	CH.STAT		status:
			0: OK
			$FF: A1 passed absolute
			$80: A1 passed relative to A6
			other negative values: waiting
$13	CH.ACTN	byte	action required for waiting job (value of D0)
$14	CH.JOBWT	long	ID of job waiting for I/O
$18	CH.END		drivers may use this area onwards

APPENDIX C
Trap Calls

Trap #1 *Page*

Trap #2   *Page*

1	IO.OPEN	open a channel	39
2	IO.CLOSE	close a channel	40
3	IO.FORMT	format a medium	41
4	IO.DELET	delete a file	42

Trap #3   *Page*

0	IO.PEND	test pending input	44
1	IO.FBYTE	fetch a byte	45
2	IO.FLINE	fetch a line	45
3	IO.FSTRG	fetch a string of bytes	46
4	IO.EDLIN	edit a line	47
5	IO.SBYTE	send a byte	47
6		not implemented (gives 'bad parameter')	
7	IO.SSTRG	send a string of bytes	48
8		not implemented	
9	SD.EXTOP	external operation (A2)	63
$0A	SD.PXENQ	read window size/cursor position (pixel)	64
$0B	SD.CHENQ	read window size/cursor position (character)	65
$0C	SD.BORDR	set window border	65
$0D	SD.WDEF	re-define window	66
$0E	SD.CURE	enable cursor	67
$0F	SD.CURS	disable cursor	67
$10	SD.POS	set cursor position	68
$11	SD.TAB	set horizontal position	68
$12	SD.NL	do newline	69
$13	SD.PCOL	set to previous column	69
$14	SD.NCOL	set to next column	69
$15	SD.PROW	set to previous row	69
$16	SD.NROW	set to next row	69
$17	SD.PIXP	set pixel position	70
$18	SD.SCROL	scroll entire window	70
$19	SD.SCRTP	scroll top of window	70
$1A	SD.SCRBT	scroll bottom of window	70
$1B	SD.PAN	pan whole window	71
$1C		not implemented (gives 'bad parameter')	
$1D		not implemented (gives 'bad parameter')	
$1E	SD.PANLN	pan cursor line	71
$1F	SD.PANRT	pan righthand side of cursor line	71
$20	SD.CLEAR	clear whole window	72
$21	SD.CLRTP	clear top of window	72
$22	SD.CLRBT	clear bottom of window	72
$23	SD.CLRLN	clear cursor line	72
$24	SD.CLRRT	clear to right of cursor	72
$25	SD.FOUNT	set character fonts	72
$26	SD.RECOL	recolour a window	74
$27	SD.SETPA	set paper colour	75
$28	SD.SETST	set strip colour	75
$29	SD.SETIN	set ink colour	75

Trap #4   *Page*

APPENDIX D
Vector Summary

Page

Page

APPENDIX E
ASCII Character Set

Dec	Hex	Character	Key combinations
Ø	Ø	NULL	CTRL £
1	1		CTRL A
2	2		CTRL B
3	3		CTRL C
4	4		CTRL D
5	5		CTRL E
6	6		CTRL F
7	7		CTRL F
8	8		CTRL G
9	9		TAB or CTRL H
10	$ØA		ENTER or CTRL J
11	$ØB		CTRL K
12	$ØC		CTRL L
13	$ØD		CTRL M
14	$ØE		CTRL N
15	$ØF		CTRL O
16	$10		CTRL P
17	$11		CTRL Q
18	$12		CTRL R
19	$13		CTRL S
20	$14		CTRL T
21	$15		CTRL U
22	$16		CTRL V
23	$17		CTRL W

24	$18		CTRL X
25	$19		CTRL Y
26	$1A		CTRL Z
27	$1B		ESC or CTRL {
28	$1C		CTRL |
29	$1D		CTRL }
30	$1E		CTRL ~
31	$1F		CTRL ©
32	$20	SPACE	
33	$21	!	
34	$22	"	
35	$23	#	
36	$24	$	
37	$25	%	
38	$26	&	
39	$27	'	
40	$28	(	
41	$29	)	
42	$2A	*	
43	$2B	+	
44	$2C	,	
45	$2D	-	
46	$2E	.	
47	$2F	/	
48	$30	0	
49	$31	1	
50	$32	2	
51	$33	3	
52	$34	4	
53	$35	5	
54	$36	6	
55	$37	7	
56	$38	8	

57	$39	9
58	$3A	:
59	$3B	;
60	$3C	<
61	$3D	=
62	$3E	>
63	$3F	?
64	$40	@
65	$41	A
66	$42	B
67	$43	C
68	$44	D
69	$45	E
70	$46	F
71	$47	G
72	$48	H
73	$49	I
74	$4A	J
75	$4B	K
76	$4C	L
77	$4D	M
78	$4E	N
79	$4F	O
80	$50	P
81	$51	Q
82	$52	R
83	$53	S
84	$54	T
85	$55	U
86	$56	V
87	$57	W
88	$58	X
89	$59	Y

90	$5A	Z
91	$5B	[
92	$5C	\
93	$5D	]
94	$5E	↑
95	$5F	_
96	$60	£
97	$61	a
98	$62	b
99	$63	c
100	$64	d
101	$65	e
102	$66	f
103	$67	g
104	$68	h
105	$69	i
106	$6A	j
107	$6B	k
108	$6C	l
109	$6D	m
110	$6E	n
111	$6F	o
112	$70	p
113	$71	q
114	$72	r
115	$73	s
116	$74	t
117	$75	u
118	$76	v
119	$77	w
120	$78	x
121	$79	y
122	$7A	z

123	$7B	{	
124	$7C	|	
125	$7D	}	
126	$7E	~	
127	$7F	©	
128	$8Ø		CTRL SPACE
129	$81	ã	CTRL !
13Ø	$82	â	CTRL "
131	$83	é	CTRL #
132	$84	ö	CTRL $
133	$85	õ	CTRL %
134	$86	ø	CTRL &
135	$87	ü	CTRL '
136	$88	ç	CTRL (
137	$89	ñ	CTRL)
138	$8A	æ	CTRL *
139	$8B	œ	CTRL +
14Ø	$8C	á	CTRL ,
141	$8D	à	CTRL -
142	$8E	â	CTRL .
143	$8F	ë	CTRL /
144	$9Ø	è	CTRL Ø
145	$91	ê	CTRL 1
146	$92	ï	CTRL 2
147	$93	í	CTRL 3
148	$94	ì	CTRL 4
149	$95	î	CTRL 5
15Ø	$96	ó	CTRL 6
151	$97	ò	CTRL 7
152	$98	ô	CTRL 8
153	$99	ú	CTRL 9
154	$9A	ù	CTRL :
155	$9B	û	CTRL ;

156	$9C	ß	CTRL <
157	$9D	¢	CTRL =
158	$9E	¥	CTRL >
159	$9F	`	CTRL ?
160	$A0	Ä	CTRL @
161	$A1	Ã	CTRL SHIFT A
162	$A2	Å	CTRL SHIFT B
163	$A3	É	CTRL SHIFT C
164	$A4	Ö	CTRL SHIFT D
165	$A5	Õ	CTRL SHIFT E
166	$A6	Ø	CTRL SHIFT F
167	$A7	Ü	CTRL SHIFT G
168	$A8	Ç	CTRL SHIFT H
169	$A9	Ñ	CTRL SHIFT I
170	$AA	Æ	CTRL SHIFT J
171	$AB	Œ	CTRL SHIFT K
172	$AC	α	CTRL SHIFT L
173	$AD	δ	CTRL SHIFT M
174	$AE	θ	CTRL SHIFT N
175	$AF	λ	CTRL SHIFT O
176	$B0	μ	CTRL SHIFT P
177	$B1	π	CTRL SHIFT Q
178	$B2	φ	CTRL SHIFT R
179	$B3	ı	CTRL SHIFT S
180	$B4	¿	CTRL SHIFT T
181	$B5	ę	CTRL SHIFT U
182	$B6	ş	CTRL SHIFT V
183	$B7	н	CTRL SHIFT W
184	$B8	«	CTRL SHIFT X
185	$B9	»	CTRL SHIFT Y
186	$BA	÷	CTRL SHIFT Z
187	$BB	←	CTRL [

188	$BC	➡	CTRL \
189	$BD	↑	CTRL]
190	$BE	↓	CTRL ↑
191	$BF	□	CTRL _
192	$C0		LEFT
193	$C1		ALT LEFT
194	$C2		CTRL LEFT
195	$C3		CTRL ALT LEFT
196	$C4		SHIFT LEFT
197	$C5		SHIFT ALT LEFT
198	$C6		SHIFT CTRL LEFT
199	$C7		SHIFT CTRL ALT LEFT
200	$C8		RIGHT
201	$C9		ALT RIGHT
202	$CA		CTRL RIGHT
203	$CB		CTRL ALT RIGHT
204	$CC		SHIFT RIGHT
205	$CD		SHIFT ALT RIGHT
206	$CE		SHIFT CTRL RIGHT
207	$CF		SHIFT CTRL ALT RIGHT
208	$D0		UP
209	$D1		ALT UP
210	$D2		CTRL UP
211	$D3		CTRL ALT UP
212	$D4		SHIFT UP
213	$D5		SHIFT ALT UP
214	$D6		SHIFT CTRL UP
215	$D7		SHIFT CTRL ALT UP
216	$D8		DOWN
217	$D9		ALT DOWN
218	$DA		CTRL DOWN
219	$DB		CTRL ALT DOWN

220	$DC	SHIFT DOWN
221	$DD	SHIFT ALT DOWN
222	$DE	SHIFT CTRL DOWN
223	$DF	SHIFT CTRL ALT DOWN
224	$E0	CAPS LOCK
225	$E1	ALT CAPSLOCK
226	$E2	CTRL CAPSLOCK
227	$E3	ALT CTRL CAPSLOCK
228	$E4	SHIFT CAPSLOCK
229	$E5	SHIFT ALT CAPSLOCK
230	$E6	SHIFT CTRL CAPSLOCK
231	$E7	SHIFT CTRL ALT CAPSLOCK
232	$E8	F1
233	$E9	CTRL F1
234	$EA	SHIFT F1
235	$EB	CTRL SHIFT F1
236	$EC	F2
237	$ED	CTRL F2
238	$EE	SHIFT F2
239	$EF	CTRL SHIFT F2
240	$F0	F3
241	$F1	CTRL F3
242	$F2	SHIFT F3
243	$F3	CTRL SHIFT F3
244	$F4	F4
245	$F5	CTRL F4
246	$F6	SHIFT F4
247	$F7	CTRL SHIFT F4
248	$F8	F5
249	$F9	CTRL F5
250	$FA	SHIFT F5
251	$FB	CTRL SHIFT F5
252	$FC	SHIFT SPACE

253	$FD	SHIFT TAB
254	$FE	SHIFT ENTER
255	$FF	(ALT)

Index

Other titles from Sunshine

Mathematics on the Commodore 64
Czes Kosniowski ISBN 0 946408 14 9 £5.95

Advanced Programming Techniques on the Commodore 64
David Lawrence ISBN 0 946408 23 8 £5.95

Commodore 64 Disk Companion
David Lawrence & Mark England ISBN 0 946408 49 1 £7.95

The Working Commodore 64
David Lawrence ISBN 0 946408 02 5 £5.95

Commodore 64 Machine Code Master
David Lawrence & Mark England ISBN 0 946408 05 X £6.95

Machine Code Games Routines for the Commodore 64
Paul Roper ISBN 0 946408 47 5 £6.95

Programming for Education on the Commodore 64
John Scriven & Patrick Hall ISBN 0 946408 27 0 £5.95

Commodore 64 Music
Ian Waugh ISBN 0 946408 78 5 £6.95

Writing Strategy Games on your Commodore 64
John White ISBN 0 946408 54 8 £6.95

COMMODORE 16/PLUS 4 BOOKS

The Working C16
David Lawrence ISBN 0 946408 62 9 £6.95

The Commodore C16/Plus 4 Companion
Brian Lloyd ISBN 0 946408 64 5 £5.95

ELECTRON BOOKS

Graphic Art for the Electron Computer
Boris Allan ISBN 0 946408 20 3 £5.95

The Working Electron
John Scriven ISBN 0 946408 52 1 £5.95

Programming for Education on the Electron Computer
John Scriven & Patrick Hall ISBN 0 946408 21 1 £5.95

BBC COMPUTER BOOKS

Functional Forth for the BBC Computer
Boris Allan ISBN 0 946408 04 1 £5.95

Graphic Art for the BBC Computer
Boris Allan ISBN 0 946408 08 4 £5.95

DIY Robotics and Sensors for the BBC Computer
John Billingsley   ISBN 0 946408 13 0   **£6.95**
Artificial Intelligence on the BBC/Electron
Keith & Steven Brain   ISBN 0 946408 36 X   **£6.95**
Essential Maths on the BBC and Electron Computer
Czes Kosniowski   ISBN 0 946408 34 3   **£5.95**
Programming for Education on the BBC Computer
John Scriven & Patrick Hall   ISBN 0 946408 10 6   **£5.95**
Making Music on the BBC Computer
Ian Waugh   ISBN 0 946408 26 2   **£5.95**

DRAGON BOOKS

Advanced Sound & Graphics for the Dragon
Keith & Steven Brain   ISBN 0 946408 06 8   **£5.95**
Artificial Intelligence on the Dragon Computer
Keith & Steven Brain   ISBN 0 946408 33 5   **£6.95**
Dragon 32 Games Master
Keith & Steven Brain   ISBN 0 946408 03 3   **£5.95**
The Working Dragon
David Lawrence   ISBN 0 946408 01 7   **£5.95**
The Dragon Trainer
Brian Lloyd   ISBN 0 946408 09 2   **£5.95**

ATARI BOOKS

Atari Adventures
Tony Bridge   ISBN 0 946408 18 1   **£5.95**
Writing Strategy Games on your Atari Computer
John White   ISBN 0 946408 22 X   **£5.95**

SINCLAIR QL BOOKS

Artificial Intelligence on the Sinclair QL
Keith & Steven Brain   ISBN 0 946408 41 6   **£6.95**
Sinclair QL Adventures
Tony Bridge & Richard Williams   ISBN 0 946408 66 1   **£5.95**
Introduction to Simulation Techniques on the Sinclair QL
John Cochrane   ISBN 0 946408 45 9   **£6.95**
Developing Applications for the Sinclair QL
Mike Grace   ISBN 0 946408 63 7   **£6.95**

Mathematics on the Sinclair QL
Czes Kosniowski   ISBN 0 946408 43 2   £6.95

The Working Sinclair QL
David Lawrence   ISBN 0 946408 46 7   £6.95

Quill, Easel, Archive & Abacus on the Sinclair QL
Alison McCallum-Varey   ISBN 0 946408 55 6   £6.95

Inside the Sinclair QL
Jeff Naylor & Diane Rogers   ISBN 0 946408 40 8   £6.95

Assembly Language Programming on the Sinclair QL
Andrew Pennell   ISBN 0 946408 42 4   £7.95

AMSTRAD BOOKS

The Working Amstrad
David Lawrence & Simon Lane   ISBN 0 946408 60 2   £5.95

GENERAL BOOKS

Home Applications on your Micro
Mike Grace   ISBN 0 946408 50 5   £6.95

Sunshine also publishes

POPULAR COMPUTING WEEKLY

The first weekly magazine for home computer users. Each copy contains Top 10 charts of the best-selling software and books and up-to-the-minute details of the latest games. Other features in the magazine include regular hardware and software reviews, programming hints, computer swap, adventure corner and pages of listings for the Spectrum, Dragon, BBC, VIC 20 and 64, ZX 81 and other popular micros. Only 40p a week, a year's subscription costs £19.95 (£9.98 for six months) in the UK and £37.40 (£18.70 for six months) overseas.

DRAGON USER

The monthly magazine for all users of Dragon microcomputers. Each issue contains reviews of software and peripherals, programming advice for beginners and advanced users, program listings, a technical advisory service and all the latest news related to the Dragon. A year's subscription (12 issues) costs £10 in the UK and £16 overseas.

COMMODORE HORIZONS

The monthly magazine for all users of Commodore computers. Each issue contains reviews of software and peripherals, programming advice for beginners and advanced users, program listings, a technical advisory service and all the latest news. A year's subscription costs £10 in the UK and £16 overseas.

For further information contact:
Sunshine
12–13 Little Newport Street
London WC2H 7PP
01-437 4343

Telex: 296275